Confessions
of a Stockbroker

Confessions
of a Stockbroker

by Brutus

Little, Brown and Company — Boston — Toronto

Published simultaneously in Canada
by Little, Brown & Company (Canada) Limited

PRINTED IN THE UNITED STATES OF AMERICA

For my father,
with love and respect

All pigs are equal
But some pigs are more equal than others . . .

— George Orwell
Animal Farm

My office is representative of countless different brokerage offices throughout the country, and its operations reflect the struggle for survival of the entire brokerage industry during the crisis year of 1970.

The characters in this book are in every case fictitious. The situations, while they are derived from my own experience, have in every instance been deliberately altered to confound, confuse and otherwise render identification of the principals impossible.

After all, the old family shoe business does not close down at three-thirty every afternoon. And besides, I cannot abide my relatives. They make me nervous.

Introduction

June 1970

Why should making money in the stock market be such a mystery? Losing money is very easy to millions of Americans. It always has been. Clients have told me on many occasions: "You want to make money in the stock market? Watch what I do . . . then do the opposite. It's guaranteed."

I have at least two hundred clients who think that they're uniquely gifted at losing money in the market. Actually they've got much more company than that. In the past sixteen months the stock market has declined some 300 points in the Dow-Jones averages. Approximately $280 billion worth of paper values have been wiped out. Two hundred eighty billion is so large a figure maybe it doesn't mean much to you. But if you've seen your $20,000 nest egg decline to less than $3,700, you know what it means. A retired grocer (is anyone a grocer anymore?) who has lost that much money said to me: "Three thousand seven hundred dollars. It might as well be nothing; that's what $3,700 is. Do I sell what I got now and put it in the bank? If I do that, it'll be the bottom of the market. Take it from me."

How do you come back from a $16,000 bath? How does the stock market recover $280 billion worth of value?

I am in a nonbusiness. Inventory is never a problem for me, yet my inventories are unlimited. Seasons are never a problem, yet style-changes in my business would give Yves St. Laurent a spastic colon. Selling my merchandise is easy because it sells itself. Dreams of glory always sell themselves. Men and women lie, cheat, steal, kill and commit suicide over my merchandise. It makes them miserable and it makes them joyous; it makes everything possible and everything impossible. If I peddled LSD, the illusions I sold could put me in jail; if I sold my body, I wouldn't last long (although there are those who love it); if I sought through politics that power I now hold over men's emotions, I could be voted out of the White House and end up scribbling my memoirs for some library yet to be built. But I can have it all. I *do* have it all and I don't even pay for my secretary or my long-distance calls. I'm a stockbroker and my game is greed.

There is no doubt about it. The stock market was *the* business to be in in the 1960's. It was wild and woolly, with go-go concepts of performance and money management, New Issue fever, record trading volume. More instant millionaires were made in the sixties than in any other decade of our history. Then, suddenly, came the "back-office crunch," the curtailed hours, the long decline, the failures. The foundations of our financial institutions were threatened with destruction. Most certainly they will undergo violent change.

Yet the 1970's promise even greater opportunities because of these changes. Knowing what we know of the past, how are we going to treat our money in the years to come? How are we going to manage it, have it work for us? Who's going to manage it properly? Who's going to run it best?

In this book, I proceed from the thesis that there will be stockbrokers as long as there is a psychic and emotional need for the kind of therapy we perform. There is, after all, something so *unsatisfying* about blaming a computer for a bad recommendation on Honeywell at 142. It will always be easier to blame your idiot nephew at Merrill Lynch or Bache or wherever, who should have gone into the family nail business in the first place. And don't tell me he went to Wharton or UCLA and majored in finance

One of the points of this book is to instruct you in making money decisions in the stock market by knowing some tricks of common sense and by learning to have a sense of humor about what makes stocks go up and down.

Before you read further, let me assure you that I make my living from commissions, in addition to managing a large branch office in a major city for a member of the New York Stock Exchange. My commission business is such that I can net $40,000 a year without coming into the office at all, and my income is not supplemented by clipping coupons on inherited bonds or waiting for the quarterly check from American Telephone that my grandfather made me promise never to sell (and which is now down 35 points in the last five years). But I *do* come into the office every day, and not just for the money but for the education. All those people with all those longings. You never know *anyone* until you have dealt with his money.

This book will take you through a pivotal six months, from June 1 to December 31, 1970, as the stock market moves in and out of the longest Bear market since the Depression. In *Confessions of a Stockbroker,* I mean to tell you how money is made and lost on a day-to-day basis; how New Issues are created and marketed and promoted; how to choose a stockbroker and how to avoid one; how and why people sell out to other companies; the truth about the Institutional Gods, the money managers with feet of clay (or an occasional touch of athlete's foot); the mutual funds; the hedge fund gunslingers; how to trade over-the-counter and escape rape; whether the back-office crunch really affects you or not; how news affects the market; and how the market affects business, politics, even the balance of international power.

In *Confessions of a Stockbroker,* you will meet the people who make this business what it is: the customer's men with your best interests at heart; the Big Producers and the journeymen who struggle to make $100 a week; the brokers who say their clients can't complain. If you want, consider it an identification game; a game of finding your own type among the hundreds of customers I talk with in the course of a year, of finding your stock among the hundreds of situations discussed, both the good ones and the "cancers."

By writing this book, I want to dispel the illusions and myths that surround the stock market and its people. I want to fill *Confessions of a Stockbroker* with the gossip and guts of what is to me the greatest game of all. For the stock market is not so frightening or magical. Nor are everyone's efforts to succeed as cursed as they may sometimes appear. Yes, Virginia, there *are* good and honest brokers, just as there are reformed prostitutes. You might learn enough here to rectify past mistakes. You may even turn a potential disaster into that most elusive of triumphs, a capital gain. At the very least you can raise some hell with your own broker.

As long as he isn't a relative.

Confessions
of a Stockbroker

1.

A Breather

Monday, June 1:

I'm usually numb on Monday mornings and it's not much consolation to know that I'm joined by millions of other Americans. But today for a change I have not been numbed by my weekend research (the Sunday *New York Times* and *Barron's*). *Barron's* particularly can throw fear into the hearts of brokers, because its articles have in the last few years had a tendency to put the kiss of death onto favorites of the glamour chasers: Cameo Parkway Records, PKL Industries, Levin Townsend Computer, National Student Marketing. Not that they didn't need killing. But did they have to desecrate the graves?

Nothing happened over the weekend to destroy the eu-

3

phoria of last week when the Dow-Jones averages went up 40 points and pulled a lot of legs off a lot of window ledges. One large brokerage house, I was told, had eighteen hundred sell-out telegrams poised to send to clients just before the rally started. Since a mass of sell-out telegrams produces panic selling, the general depression in stocks continues to feed on itself. At least we had had a respite with the rally, but everyone was holding his breath.

I hate having visitors early in the day. Visitors are bad in a brokerage office; they spoil your concentration. (When the tickers are moving, I suppose it's equally disconcerting for the customer to have a broker looking over his shoulder at the prices.) In fact, it has always bothered me to have visitors so early. I remember one old lady with a Bonwit's bag full of Sears, Roebuck stock that she had had since 1933, who was referred to me by a client of mine, her doctor. She was in the office at the dot of ten. She discussed her problem, was ready to sell, but jumped up suddenly. "Young man," she said, "when I do business with someone, I expect him to look me in the eye." She left, clutching the Bonwit's bag, and I never could explain to her that I was acting in her best interests, studying the ticker tape for the last price of Sears. Of course, that was in the days before the desk-top quote machines. I've been around for a while.

Two visitors were waiting for me this morning: one old friend from college who happened to be in town and one young man named Norman whom I had been senior adviser to in boarding school. Norman was with his fiancée. He was pimply-faced when I knew him and known to abuse himself a good deal. Evidently his fiancée had straightened him out because he was tall, clear-faced and happy. Norman's father owned a filter manufacturing company and had sold out to an air pollution devices firm that was public. His father received stock in return. It was now 6. Norman, on his father's advice, had bought 300 shares in the open market at 53⅞, the all-time high. Norman now needed the money to take his girl to Acapulco on a prenuptial tryout and had to dump his stock to pay the fares. His father still believed it would be 100 someday and faith is a wonderful thing.

You will find that the smartest businessmen, who run the tightest corporate ships, consistently lose money in the stock market and know nothing about what makes value in securities. *Emotion* makes value. A stock is only worth what somebody else will pay at a given moment. Someone buying an Andy Warhol Campbell's soup can creation for $500 to put in an adorable beach house at Fire Island might be amazed to discover that there will be a time when the painting won't bring $17.50. Likewise, he will hope against hope that the 100 shares he bought at 50 and which dropped to 10 will recover in the near future. Also, yesterday's heroes almost never recover: the bowling stocks; the vending machine stocks; the franchisers; the semiconductors; the airlines; the color TV manufacturers; the tulip bulbs of the 1700's; the Davy Crockett hats of the 1950's; the hula hoops.

I have an ivory Mah-Jongg set that was given to me as a curiosity. I'm curious about it. Look out when today's glamours go down. Just because they're low, they are not necessarily cheap. The girl who got into your bed a princess at midnight, appears without makeup in the morning a frog. All you feel is hangover and remorse. The same is true of yesterday's heroes. Do yourself a favor and make the divorce painless. Do not be married to your stocks; do not fall in love with fads to the extent that you are unable to part with them. We'll talk a lot about how and when to cut losses. As for fads — there'll be new ones every year. We never run out of inventory.

Anyway, I sold Norman's 300 shares of his air pollution stock and also hustled my old college friend out as quickly as possible. He had just opened an office for temporary help and I told him that I'd call if he left his card. "I've already got temporary help," I said, "and they're here permanently." Secretaries in stock market dog days are much too busy with paperback editions of *The Love Machine* and fat, magazine crossword-puzzle books. They have so little respect for the brokers in our office who are scratching out the minimum wage that they resent taking messages or giving quotes. I send them out for coffee a lot and sometimes they treat everybody. Things have been bad.

Mail delivery since the strike has been slow. The *Wall Street Journal* doesn't usually arrive until shortly before ten, and the resident partner has called the postal supervisor three times without satisfaction. Since we are in a service business, the mail delay can make a real difference to our clients' investment programs.

Part of being a good broker is keeping current. I often clip pertinent items from the Dow-Jones news ticker or the *Wall Street Journal* to send to my clients who have interests in particular items. Give your broker a prod in this direction; don't wait for annual reports. By then it's usually too late. The last annual of National Student Marketing made you want to become a stockbroker so badly you felt unpatriotic if you weren't. It screamed "Youth is a consumer. Buy me!" so much you were covered by the message like Muzak at the dentist's. But financials were somehow obscured and the stock thereafter dropped from 35 to 1. Annual reports are pretty but it's the numbers that count. Have someone explain them to you.

The market was strong this morning with good volume and good buying. It was strange to hear the phones ring again after so many months of watching my brokers playing with themselves. The public is in this market like they're afraid they might be missing out on something and maybe they will be. There are dozens of companies, *good* companies which, if they are liquidated today, would bring more per share *on liquidation* than they sell for in the market. Why is this? The stock market can be counted on to overreact in both directions. When times are good, prices go much higher than anyone thinks they will. The reverse is true when times are bad. Why has the market been so slow from September 1969 to May 1970? One big reason is this: a lot of large *and* small investors liked a stock at 40 in the spring of 1969 but it seemed too high. When it dropped to 30 in the summertime they bought it. It looked cheap. They averaged their position (bought more) at 20 in the fall. It looked like a steal. Now it's 8, 9, 10, or 11 and the customer is "locked into his stock." He won't sell; it's too low. He won't buy more. Either he has no more money or he's frightened. Possibly both. And his own business is now turning

7

sour. This is the case with hundreds of stocks and thousands of stockholders. Despite Washington's predictions of firming business trends and success in fighting inflation toward the end of 1970, the average investor *knows* we've been in a recession for three or four months and *his* business is lousy.

Good stock markets feed on themselves when people are loose. People are tight now, and even if they have money, they're afraid to spend it. So the stockbrokers bring their lunches in Baggies: leftover lamb sandwiches with mint jelly for the young men who send out for bouillon in cups; carrot sticks and hard-boiled eggs for the dieters. The resident partner goes out for a shrimp cocktail and Gibson on the rocks and worries about clerical salaries and computers and Exchange capital requirements and his own dwindling share of money in the firm. Two years ago we were closing one day a week and at two P.M. the rest of the time to discourage heavy trading that we could not keep up with. This year we worked on Memorial Day and I made the men call old accounts, attempting to light some fires. "Everybody's away," they told me. "It's Memorial Day." Memorial Day for everybody's stocks.

Many brokers are very lazy. That's why they become brokers. As a class of people, taken on the whole, they are the most ignorant of any profession. A generalization? I defy anyone to get into a room full of brokers and not come away agreeing with me. Ask a broker sometime what stocks are in *his* portfolio. Nobody ever asks that. Most brokers I know own very few stocks. And I've seen my office turn over completely six times in ten years.

This week the firm eliminated the current training program in a cost-cutting move, firing a dozen candidates for registration. The partners are all in danger of seeing their capital eliminated and are doing everything they can to lower the break-even point. Costs in the industry have risen tenfold in seven years. And our selling price has remained the same since 1958.

We are trying to gear the firm's operations to an 8-million-share day average on the New York Stock Exchange, meaning that we should show a profit on everything over 8 million shares. Good luck. There's so much dead wood on Wall Street that a spark from a Morgan partner's English Oval would set off a conflagration from the Battery to City Hall that would take Smokey the Bear years to reconstruct. Every day three or four unemployed account executives apply for positions with us. An institutional salesman from another house came in today wearing a winter suit and vest. They were paying him $22,000 a year plus unlimited expenses to call upon certain mutual funds and banks that they had chosen. His single purpose was to romance the funds and peddle his firm's research suggestions. He was personable, had the right credentials, and every single opinion he had was straight from *Time*. He was looking to make a switch; the heat was on at his firm to produce. He had three children and in 1968 bought three acres of vacation property with a dream to build a redwood house like ones he had seen many times in *House Beautiful*. The man was unemployable. I wouldn't give him house room, let alone *House Beautiful*. There are hundreds like him who will be out of jobs on Wall Street. Probably the big banks will end up taking many of these people. They'll pay them $11,500 a year and bury them in the trust departments. It's scary.

A small hedge fund called, friends of mine who manage $2 million. Hedge funds differ from mutual funds in the sense that they are distinctly unregulated; operate with relatively little money; can go long, sell short, or write options. The managers of a hedge fund take 20 per cent of the profits *if* there are profits. (Twenty per cent of nothing is nothing.) These funds have sprung up like toadstools in the last two years. They seemed the foolproof way to get rich in a bull market: buy something a lot of other funds bought, go along for the ride, get out and skim 20 per cent off the top.

My friends were fully invested on the *long* side all during 1969 when the market declined almost steadily the entire year. Most hedge funds were long all year. Or if they were short, they covered too soon. Nervous in the service. Now they were going short like mad trying to catch up, in almost anything they could find that was selling over fifty times their projected year's earnings. They sold 400 H & R Block (the tax consultants) short at 44½. Block looked much too high to them, selling at a generous multiple and seemingly overlooked in the Bear market.

Remember this about Bear markets: bears are hungry. They get around to everything at the picnic. If you own a stock that holds like a rock though everything else seems to be going to hell, think about getting out. They'll find you eventually. Three mutual funds own 150,000 shares of Block. If they decide to sell, it'll be 27½ before you can say Milton Friedman. I think Block is a great short myself; their earnings have increased steadily but I look for a lot of little people next year to do their own tax returns. The stock does not deserve to sell in the 40's. But my hedge fund needs a miracle to save them. The net asset value (they started with $2 million) is $450,000, and they're operating from one of the manager's apartments. They used to have a suite of offices and a receptionist who was only kept on for the two managers, who would have her during lunch hour in sequence, one day one, the next the other. She disappeared along with the suite of offices when they broke their lease. Twenty per cent of nothing is nothing.

H & R Block looks like such a good idea I shorted 100 for myself at 44⅜ (after my customers' orders had been filled) and left for the day to speak to a luncheon meeting of a women's investment club. They were all weight watchers and I felt like a small steak but settled for what they served: hard-boiled-egg wedges, tuna salad and iced coffee with Sweeta. We ate on tray tables in the well-lit library of the club president's home. If you want my advice on investment clubs: forget them. They're a waste of time for practically everyone concerned unless you use them *strictly* for the learning process. Most of them are too big. Ideally, they should be limited to ten members. Most such clubs begin ambitiously but never get off the ground. If women had been in the negotiations at Panmunjom, the Korean War would still be on. With apologies to Women's Liberation movements — I'm all for them. Individual woman investors are sometimes much better suited emotionally for stock trading and they're *much* better short sellers than men are. They *love* to see companies go into chapter eleven of the bankruptcy act.

And there's nothing like a walk around the corner during lunchtime in a Bear market counting girls without bras. It restores my faith in free enterprise.

Investment clubs should have a revolving committee (that changes every three months) to make the decisions. The other members *and* their broker should only be advisory sounding boards. This narrows the hassle down to three people and everyone eventually gets a crack at it.

"You put us into that Avnet at 33," one of the women said to another.

"My husband played golf with the owner at the Palm Beach Country Club. *He* said it was a good buy."

"He's dead now."

"So are we in the stock," said another woman. Avnet was selling today at 7½.

Recriminations took an hour, with me as moderator trying to keep things from getting ugly. I left at two-fifteen with orders to sell, the next day, 75 Polaroid ("to take a profit, finally"), 50 Johnson & Johnson ("ditto"), and 100 Avnet ("to take a loss and balance out the gains"). I was going to buy them 100 Itek at 36½, whose financial picture I like, and 1,000 Originala, the finest manufacturer of quality women's coats in the country. (Originala looks awfully cheap to me at 4½. No doubt a good cash position, good earning potential when the economy turns, and paying dividends at a current rate of 6½ per cent per year. And the stock down from 30 two years ago. Perhaps it's not worth 30 but I think I can double their money in it in a year.)

The investment club is a healthy one, latest valuation being slightly over $65,000. Why do I bother with ladies'

investment clubs? This year I bother. Mostly because
their husbands all have money. They all invest or specu-
late in the stock market. In a bad year, everyone hates his
broker and there will be a lot of switching around. It's a
hell of a lot simpler to shed stockbrokers than to shed
wives. I'll have a lot of new accounts by the end of 1970.
If there's an end to 1970. Some people aren't sure.

The Dow-Jones averages closed at 710.38. Up 9.92.
There was still some room to move.

Tuesday, June 2:

The market was quiet most of the day. "Consolidat-
ing," the analysts call it. Whenever it's quiet I try to
chat with the customer's men in the office to see if they
have any problems and to exchange ideas. We have four-
teen brokers in our branch office, sixteen counting the
resident partner and myself; two secretaries; one bookkeeper, who can fill in anywhere; and two order-room
people, one male, one female, who relieve each other all
day on the Teletype and the phones to the over-the-counter
dealers.

Jim Curran is a red-headed Irishman with a tongue like
the snakes St. Patrick was supposed to have driven out.
He's one of our customer's men and he sits in the back
row of desks. His major account is the endowment
portfolio of one of the largest Jesuit colleges in America.
A classmate of Curran's is the chief portfolio manager at
the college and feeds Jim this business and the substantial
commissions involved. Jim reciprocates by getting fifty-
yard-line tickets for his classmates to Army–Navy games,

Boston College–Holy Cross games and Notre Dame–Ohio State games. They go together and get stinko, pretend to be alumni of the side they were sitting with and spend the weekend at fraternity houses or dormitories singing "If You're Irish, Come into the Parlor" and chasing girls from Manhattanville, Newton College of the Sacred Heart and Randolph-Macon (but only the Catholic girls from Randolph-Macon). Jim Curran received $50,000 in gross commissions last year from the endowment fund's trading. He netted 35 per cent of that figure, or about $17,500, from that one account. He was a bachelor and didn't bother pursuing other business very actively. If it came in, fine. But he never went out of his way. This is the kind of broker you love to have working for you. He makes no decisions himself, merely accepts orders directed to him. He makes no waves, runs up no extensive phone bills, keeps his major account supplied with gifts of wine, dinners and tickets. He is utterly profitable for us.

But since no relationship is perfect, and since Jim has no responsibilities, he zings the other brokers when he's bored. He's full of statistics and trivial information. Watching the ticker tape this morning, he commented, "The Church says about the two-week rally that you can't change objectives in such a short time. Meanwhile the market recovered from 650 to 710 in four days. They say they're bearish. And they get the word from Christ Himself." Still watching the tape: "Do you know that I heard the average customer's loss around the country in the last year is $10,000 apiece?"

"No kidding," he was told. "I believe it."

"And did you know that the Catholic Church has veto power over the *Encyclopaedia Britannica?*"

"Never mind that. What stocks does the Church like?"

"They like Syntex at 23."

"Syntex?"

"Sure. The Pill. Important manufacturer of the Pill. If we're in the market we must know what we're doing. You-know-Who's on our side." Jim Curran doesn't deserve to be Irish. He has no respect.

A customer called me from Paris, where he had gone to deliver a paper titled "Children's Spring-Summer Allergies in the Northeastern United States." Only a doctor will call collect from wherever he is and only a doctor will take so much advantage of travel-entertainment loopholes that the Tax Code provides. Dr. Max Easton, the allergist, has quite a racket. The reception room at his office looks like the unemployment-compensation line at Cape Kennedy: people queuing up for rapid-fire shots, in and out, $25 a pop. I felt no compunction about recommending that the doctor turn over his portfolio frequently. Nobody else ever gets back at him. And he helps it along by never being able to sit in a stock for more than a month. He loses some money every year, but we have a good relationship and I know he needs the therapy.

Next to stockbrokers, business-oriented doctors are the dumbest people with money alive. The only medical hint I shall give in this office is: do not accept treatment from doctors who interrupt office hours to phone their stockbrokers. They cannot possibly concentrate on you. Dentists are almost as bad, except a dentist is not as likely to kill you. Dr. Easton bought 500 Originala at 4⅝ and

500 Occidental Petroleum at 17. "They tell me in Paris," he said, "that even without Libya and those goddamn Arabs, OXY will earn over $2 a share. It's a great company. Buy me 500." He was talking very loud so I was sure he was in some brokerage office near the Place Vendôme with lots of people listening. I put in the orders. He had made $3,000 in Occidental two years before. He loves to beat old horses to death. The name of the president of Occidental is Armand Hammer. Any company with a president named Armand Hammer can't be all bad.

Donald Counts is a broker in our office with a rich father-in-law who lives in New Jersey, where he used to manufacture paper plates, fine paper plates. He sold his business to St. Regis Paper years ago and now dabbles in investments and collects dividends at $1.60 a share on his St. Regis stock, which he will never sell. "It's like the Rock of Gibraltar," he says. "I sell out my life's blood, I don't take no funny money in return. I want to sleep nights." He currently owns 50,000 shares of Asamera Oil on the American Stock Exchange, at an average of 3¼. The stock had been as high last year as 43⅝, and Donald's father-in-law had a paper profit of $2 million. He called management every week to pester them; he called other large shareholders; he called mutual funds who owned the stock; he called oil people from other companies to check rumors. He knew more about the oil business in general and Indonesian oil in particular than any other former paper plate manufacturer in the country. He rode it up to 43⅝; down to 6¼ two weeks ago and *never* sold a share. Donald Counts, his son-in-law, is going bald and has an ulcer. He drinks milk for lunch with cups of Campbell's cream of tomato soup. Asamera more than doubled in a week during the market surge of May 20–28, from 6¼ to 14. "They're bringing up sludge," Donald says, "nearing oil on their biggest well in history. When the news is announced the stock is good for the low 20's."

I asked him, "Why didn't you buy more for customers when it was 7, 8, and 9?"

"I don't have any customers left," he said and looked ashamed.

You can have the richest father-in-law in the world for a client, but if he doesn't trade you don't make a nickel. Donald knows his father-in-law will end up taking a loss in Asamera. That's why he eats cream of tomato soup for lunch.

Wednesday, June 3, and Thursday, June 4:

I am testing a theory about recouping heavy losses of the last year. It can most successfully be done in a cheap stock, selling at $10 or under and concentrating in that stock. It must be bought heavily and continued to be bought to the exclusion of other stocks. If you show five or more stocks in your portfolio, with a substantial loss in each, consider taking the loss and lumping all the funds in one new security. The American Exchange these days looks like a grab bag of $6, $7, $8 and $9 stocks that seven months ago were all 20, 30, 40, and 50. Some of them will never come back; others should double in the next year. A lot of money can be recovered this way, but you must be selective; the odds can be cut down, however, on "cheapies." Buy companies with relatively strong balance sheets, little or no debt, and as much cash as possible. Cash has fallen upon bad times until recently. Not ever a dirty word, it just wasn't chic; it was old-fashioned. Now very few have it and there is a liquidity crisis in many executive suites.

Here's a short list of the companies (there are dozens) in the "cheapie" category (under 20). I've been buying them all. Noted are the approximate current price, the high of the last two years, and the 1970 low.

EXCHANGE	COMPANY	CURRENT	HIGH SINCE 1968	1970 LOW
ASE	Originala	4½	30	4½
NYE	Dennison Mfg.	12½	80	11
ASE	Unitrode	5	24½	4½
NYE	American Sterilizer	16	43	13
NYE	American Bakeries	10	33	8⅛
ASE	Barry Wright	7½	29	7
ASE	Financial General	10	30	9½
NYE	Cudahy Packing	10	26	9½

I do not expect them to regain the old highs for a long while, if ever. But in merely playing the numbers, I do expect to double my money within a year. I've never known a more favorable time since 1932 to concentrate on cheaper stocks. And, in this siege of depressed values, you will *not* sacrifice quality. This month will represent, historically, one of the greatest moments to make a fortune any of us will see. But the trouble with stocks, unlike real estate or diamonds or stamps or paintings, is that you can see the quoted price of your stock every day. That's what makes the difference; most people cannot stand that dreadful knowledge.

Putting the theory to work I committed sacrilege by selling 100 IBM at 282 for a client today, a swinger who owns a dating bar. He lost $12,000 in trading last year. We bought 3,000 Thiokol Chemical between 8½ and 8⅞. They're a strong company that used to sell as high as 70. Seven institutions own almost 200,000 shares, and I bought it for a fund as recently as three months ago at 11. We'll see 13 this year at least, and I'll bail my boy out, starting fresh with the twelve grand recouped. What about IBM? I don't see it going up to 120 points in the next year. We can always buy it back. *Never idolize a stock so much that you cannot bring yourself to sell it.* They're only little pieces of paper, and when we go onto punch cards there won't even be mammoth naked ladies on the certificates. For the most part, you will *never* meet an officer of a company you own shares in; for most of the companies you own you'll never even be able to give the *name* of an officer, or where their corporate head quarters is located, or what their sales are, or what their debt structure is, or even what three of their major products are. All you care about is where it closed that day.

Let's not kid ourselves. I'm not writing this book for the theorists who will drum "investigate before you invest" into your heads. The vast majority never investigate and never will. And if they did, they'd probably never buy a share of stock. This book is for the honestly unrealistic millions who are playing an unrealistic game. All they want is a stock that goes up 100 per cent in a year, pays an 8 per cent dividend while they wait, and has built-in guarantees against loss. Something conservative.

Wednesday the market was up 4.25 with little action, but Thursday my Originala started to pop. It opened at 4⅝ and got as high as 6⅛ on the highest volume in months. There was a misprint on the tape at 6⅞ and I could feel my palms itch. You never buy enough when a stock is going up; 100 shares is 100 shares too many when it goes against you. But the 6⅞ was a misprint; actually it was 5⅞. I felt like an idiot because when I saw it move I yelled to everyone in the boardroom, "I told you someone would grab that company. A sitting duck. Thin stock; it can move like hell."

A woman customer of mine was sitting with me, a real bitch whose husband had made a fortune on KLM when the airlines were hot, only to die and have his wife convert it into diamonds and Norman Norells. She had married another rich one who made a score in Litton Industries and she was doing her best to convert that score to diamonds and Puccis. Which she better do quickly, since Litton *was* 120 and I can see it going by now at 19.

My customer came in every three months to buy companies she had unemotionally researched, but she only bought stocks in this category: scientific-oriented firms, over-the-counter, with Gentile scientists and Jewish comptrollers. How she found them I'll never know, but she invariably had two or three of them for me to check out. "Nobody's gonna buy Originala this fall," she announced. "Nobody's gonna buy $300 and $400 coats. Not with the confusion over lengths and the depression on and everything." (She called it a depression because she had Litton.) "You couldn't *give* me a rag stock today." She kept crossing and uncrossing her legs, but I don't particularly care for yellow panty-hose.

The rally is losing steam and rolling at the top. Prices closed generally down, off 7.32 on the Dow. Originala was 5⅜ and I decided not to buy a pair of $60 Bally boots I had been lusting after.

Friday, June 5:

The phones are out this morning and the partner felt a little sick. He rushed out to a pay booth to call H. I. Romnes, the president of American Telephone and Telegraph. "You'll find it's much more effective to get through to the top than to call a supervisor," he's fond of saying. "Whenever you want something," he says, "call the president. You'll get action." He has the personal phone numbers of one hundred and seventeen chief executives. "It extended to my dealings with women when I was young," he goes on. "I was always bold. Came right out with what I had on my mind. Got my face slapped a lot. But I got laid a lot, too. Be brash. Be brash." I do all the hiring of secretaries but the partner has the final say.

The partner has an interesting method of trading stocks, one that often works: notice a favorite listed stock of yours, preferably one with some quality, that is, and thinly capitalized (few shares outstanding or in relatively short supply). Watch the range it trades on rallies in the market, and its range on dips. Recently Cenco Instruments, on the Big Board, has moved from 21 to 25 three times in three weeks. Place a buy order at 21¼ or near the bottom of the range. If you buy it, immediately place a sell order at 24½ or 24⅜. I've turned this stock three times in three weeks, making approximately 10 per cent on my money each time. That's about all you can expect in this narrow trading market. But if the summer goes as I expect, I might turn Cenco six or seven or eight different occasions. Eventually, the stock will move away from me, either too low (and I would not carry it under 20, thus limiting my loss) or too high. In which case I find another one. Last fall I traded Dennison Manufacturing on this basis *seven* times between 20 and 30 before it finally collapsed. That's very cheap now at 14. One of my picks in the "under 15" class. It was 55 a year ago.

Another of my customer's men, an ex advertising-media rep (they're all of the same ilk) came in with five customer statements for me to interpret. It's incredible that stockbrokers cannot read their clients' statements. It's bad enough that customers can't read them. After you open an account with a brokerage house, immediately ask your representative to interpret *his* firm's method of statement presentation. Make sure *you* understand, and what's more, that *he* understands it completely. It will save you aggravation later on. If your broker cannot read your monthly statement, how do you expect him to analyze companies for you?

Michael, my ex media rep, says, "I'm not a bookkeeper; I'm a lover." All I know is, he grossed $1,000 last month in commissions. That's net to him $350 *before* deductions. He'd *better* be a lover, because we're not going to carry stiffs forever in this market where there are brokerage firms losing as much as $100,000 *a day*.

The market is declining sharply, finishing down 11.50, which puts it under 700 for the week. "Thailand just put all their troops on full alert," said one of our tape watchers.

"All one hundred and twenty-five of 'em," said Jim Curran. "And North Korea probably sank a sampan flying the American flag."

Michael the ad man said, "After people read their *New York Times* Sunday — Nixon, Israel, Cambodia, Thailand — they'll be selling stocks on Monday morning. It'll hit the fan."

I had to agree with him. All I could think of was one of the Comtes de Rothschild's nineteenth-century advice to someone who asked him how he made his money on the Bourse. "When the streets of Paris are running with blood," he said, "I buy."

I try thinking of that a lot.

2.

Dog Days
In a Bear Market

Monday, June 8:

A client just called me. "I have a feeling of doom," he said. "But I'm usually wrong." He's been consulting a woman astrologer who put him into real estate investment trusts, which are down 20 to 30 per cent. She then advised him to ease out and start accumulating building-materials stocks, which will be very big when the new housing boom starts in 1971. We've been waiting for this new housing boom for five years and it has yet to materialize. But since *my* client's situation has something to do with Mercury's juxtaposition to Cassiopeia's Chair, he bought 300 Johns-Manville at 29½.

With the phones not ringing I have lots of time to look at the backs of the heads of my sales force and get depressed wondering what they're going to do for a living once they leave the brokerage business. I want you to understand how to choose a stockbroker when you finish this book, and I'm beginning with descriptions of *my* people. This is probably a representative sampling of the kinds of brokers in every office. Call them Registered Representatives or Customer's Men or Account Executives or whatever makes you feel that you've got the real thing. I'm eternally optimistic and call them my Sales Force. And they're getting on each other's nerves. Few of them come in before quarter to ten in the morning. It makes the days shorter and makes the silence of the phones not seem so endless. Pools are formed on the day's volume, on who writes the most orders (or the least), with quarters put into the pot. A year ago it might have been a $1 pool; two years ago, $2. Now there are brokers who will not throw in the quarter.

The man from Trans-Jet comes in to adjust the New York and American stock exchange tickers. His adjustment will eliminate the clatter and whirr of the machines. Some of the brokers complain because there is no noise at all to remind them that they are working. Stockbrokers are getting on each other's nerves.

One of my men talks to nobody else in the office except me — and to me only reluctantly. He believes that everyone is out to steal his ideas. He's Evander Wood, our Institutional man, and he locks his desk every night, his key connected to a long chain attached to his belt. Evander is a chartist — or technician, a term he prefers because it sounds more professional. In 1968 he grossed $160,000 in commissions; in 1969, a respectable $90,000. He deals strictly with institutions — mutual funds, insurance companies, trust departments of banks — giving them statistical proof of stock groups that are strong and individual companies in these groups which should be purchased. He has a gimmick, as all successful institutional men must have if their contacts are not purely social. (That is, your roommate from St. Mark's who does the buying for Mass. Investors Growth Fund or your fraternity brother from Deke at UCLA who directs Lockheed's pension fund). Judging by Evander's personality, people have to be either intimidated by his charts (he makes a poor personal impression) or so confused by his system that they buy in self-defense. He has a magic divisor that changes in relation to the volume of the market going up (upside volume) and going down (downside volume) placed in juxtaposition to his own index of glamour stocks, plus what the small buyer (odd-lotter) was selling short on a given day. Could you follow that? I never could, but Evander Wood has had fifteen mutual funds who have given him business on the basis of his information. Which proves that you can indeed fool most of the people most of the time when it comes to their money.

I've always thought Evander would be an ideal star as the tailor in "The Emperor's New Clothes," who wove beautiful threads out of nothing. When he speaks, he speaks only in charting language, referring to people in the street as having "sloping head and shoulders," to bald men as having "topped out," to broad-beamed women as pos-

sessing "descending channels" or "falling wedges." He used
to laugh and laugh at his own jokes and take orders for
5,000, 10,000, 15,000 shares at a clip. Everyone in the
office hated him; especially after he took an order. He was
a familiar figure in the financial districts, plodding along
with his pipe, his professorial air and his large briefcase
filled with charts and magic potions. He'd pick the soft-
drink industry for action and Coca-Cola in particular "for
a breakout." Then he'd sell it to the funds on the basis of
his number studies. At lunch he'd have a corned beef on
rye and a Tab. "What is this junk," he'd say suddenly,
spitting the Tab into an ashtray.

"That's Tab," I'd tell him. "Made by Coca-Cola. You
recommended it."

Then he'd get red in the face and yell: "I *never* know
what products *my* companies make. I don't know what my
companies do or where my companies are or who runs my
companies." Louder and louder he'd say, "What I care
about is — are my companies going up? Who cares what
they make?"

Evander hasn't written an order in two months and
we've taken him off his $1,000-a-month draw. He has the
desperate look in his eyes of the man who is interviewing
other firms and can't get a job. Portfolio managers who
gave him business are now explaining why their net asset
values are down as much as 40 per cent this year and
Evander has added more charts to his briefcase and more
keys to his ring. I caught a fleeting glimpse of a copy of
Samuelson's *Economics* in his top drawer before he
slammed it shut.

A year ago I was romancing a mutual fund with $100 million in assets and was taken on a tour of their offices. "This is our War Room," I was told, being led into an almost totally dark area with gun-metal gray walls and rea leather upholstery. Dominating one wall was an electronic board — the New York and American stock exchange tickers — next to a map of the world illuminated by spotlights, with the legend TODAY AMERICA — TOMORROW . . . ! Tucked in a corner of the opposite side of the room was a glassed-in cage, reminiscent of the box in which Adolf Eichmann was isolated during his trial. There was a little man inside, a young man with long sideburns, staring at the tape and holding the kind of pencil passed out to you when you took the college boards. "That's our in-house chartist," I was told. "He hasn't moved in three days but when he does you buy. We outbid five other firms to get him and had to give seventy grand plus a piece of the action." I watched him for seven minutes and he didn't even blink. It was two-fifteen.

"If he doesn't move by the close," I told them, "he's dead." They were irritated at me for saying that and I never did any business with them. I understand the in-house chartist is now doing phone surveys for the Nielsen ratings at $8,200 a year. Chartists, in most cases, need help going to the bathroom. If you have a broker who tells you, "such and such looks good on the chart," it's time for another broker.

Herbert was with us for seven years, and every day he ate a Swiss cheese sandwich on dark rye, which he brought from home. That's not so bad. I ate peanut butter and marshmallow fluff every day for *six* years in grammar school until I started to break out and my mother was convinced it was the fluff.

Herbert specialized in over-the-counter stocks. Cheap over-the-counter stocks, and all his clients would try to chisel eighths and quarters of points in runaway Bull markets and eventually end up paying 2 and 3 points higher. The biggest buyers and money managers buy and sell "at the market," at the best available current price. Are you going to be a big shot and squeeze for eighths? If you want a stock, buy it. A partner in one of the largest investment banking firms on Wall Street told me once, "You want to be a pisher? Put bids in a quarter below the market. You'll be a pisher all your life."

Herbert's customers drove him crazy. He has a spastic colon that the Swiss cheese didn't help, but he netted $12,000 a year for 1966, 1967, and 1968, more than enough to support himself and his wife and buy thousands of shares of $1 and $2 stocks that in his opinion were undervalued. Especially titanium stocks. He felt that titanium (symbol Ti, atomic weight 48.1) was *the* magic metal of the future. He would spend twenty minutes on a pitch to his dentist on titanium to get a 50-share order. His clients would nickel-dime him to death but he persevered until this year, with his two suits: one winter, one summer, both black. All of his spare money went into cheap $1 and $2 stocks, over-the-counter. Now all his dollar stocks are selling for pennies or are in chapter eleven, and even his dentist doesn't call. One day Herbert didn't come in and the mail brought his resignation and a request to approve him for unemployment compensation. His desk stays unoccupied and the partner immediately had his call director removed.

The small investor is buried, and brokers like Herbert are lining up at Prudential and Allstate looking for training in sales. But when I assembled Herbert's accounts and passed them out among my registered reps, I urged them to snatch victory from the jaws of defeat.

"What are you giving me?" Jim Curran asked after contacting some of these leads.

"I only gave you Catholic accounts," I said. "What's wrong?"

"One woman is sending me seventeen certificates in *her* name to change to *joint* name with her son. She has 7 to 12 shares of each of the companies and she wanted an opinion on each one."

"We can't afford any bad will now," I cautioned.

"I *gave* her opinions. She said, 'I can't promise any business now. Things are too low. But I surely will light a candle for you.' Don't give me any more Catholic accounts."

Does the small investor stand a chance? Or is he doomed forever to have his calls referred to Herbert? (By the way, the small investor is *not* being squeezed out of the market by costs. This is a myth. Our industry has not changed its selling price in over ten years. No other service-based industry in the country can even come close to that assertion.) The small investor is shaking the same dice as the big boys, rolling the same little ball onto the wheel. I think that's what Sylvia Porter says. If the small investor would get over the stigma of being small, he would solve a lot of his problems. Hair can be transplanted; noses can be bobbed; silicone can assist even women who don't want to make their breasts move counterclockwise in tune to Sly and the Family Stone on record at a bottomless joint in Los Angeles.

For the person who buys stocks in 10- or 50-share units: buy what you like or what your broker recommends and ask that your stock be sent to you as soon as possible so that you will receive financial reports and dividends directly from the company. Then, don't lose track of your broker; but don't harass him either. If you call once a month to check on news, progress, or just for reassurance, that's enough. Your call is not a bother if he learns to expect it at a certain time each month. (During a full moon is not bad.) Brokers can be conditioned to salivate just like Pavlov's dogs. They are always ready to do so. Expecting a once-a-month checkup, the broker will be more tolerant, easier to reach and probably receptive even to questions he may think foolish. *Don't let this habit slide; do it even if it's painful. Treat it like a Pap test. You'll stay on top of your investment situation in a healthy, constructive way.* The nervous holders who call their brokers three times a day, five days a week are the ones most apt to have their accounts turned over just to make such frequent conversation pay. Psychiatrists get $35 an hour on average. We have our little hang-ups also and most of us enjoy getting back at certain patients who use us as sounding boards for their own psyches. For the 20-share buyers: play your stockbroker as you would a neighbor you were having an affair with — once a month will keep you *both* interested.

We have a woman broker who is pure poison, from her expensive hairdo to her $60 Andrew Gellers made outside Florence, Italy. Roz the Ruthless, we call her, and a greater salesman God hath not wrought since Professor Harold Hill sold band instruments to the kids of River City, Iowa. Roz has all the vices: she smokes Lucky Strikes like the early Mike Hammer, drinks martinis for lunch, sips seven paper cups of black coffee a day, and uses four-letter words. "F——k Nixon," she'll say, never taking her eyes off the ticker, "he's killing the country. This is the Nixon market." But she also said, "F——k Johnson. He's killing the country, giving it away." And "F——k Kennedy," she said after JFK's confrontation with Roger Blough of U.S. Steel. But Eisenhower she loved, because he had kept her brother at a desk typing stencils in London in 1944 instead of sending him to Normandy.

Roz can survive the Bear market. Her grandfather owned one of the largest chains of supermarkets in the Midwest and her husband makes deals with Roz's share of the estate. Every deal her husband makes turns out well, although people pretend not to believe him. "We know Roz has you on an allowance. You never made a nickel on your own," his friends tell him. They call him Odd Job, a cruel nickname, because he is big with a tendency to narrow his eyes when he smells money. The fact that no one believes his deals drives Odd Job wild, and he takes half-page ads in local newspapers and he once rented billboards on a major throughway saying TO SAM AND THE BOYS: LATEST FINDER'S FEE — $300,000. EAT YOUR HEARTS OUT!

Roz gets back at Odd Job's friends by calling them incessantly and bullying them to buy stocks as if she were down to her last Galanos. Whatever the firm's research department puts out she attempts to push, spewing the statistics directly off the report. This is the kind of salesperson Avon Products wants; she could be Welcome Wagon's Woman of the Year.

Roz's problem is that the job stops with the sale. Seldom does she keep decent records; seldom does she follow through with a request from a client that does not end with a commission. After I bailed her out of a problem for the fiftieth time this year, I confronted her with the fact that a good stockbroker must be much more than a salesperson. "Oh yeah?" she said. "Where does it say Junior Executive dresses down Big Producer?" (Not many of her expressions were original, Marshall McLuhan would be pleased to note). "I'm paid to move the merchandise," she went on. "You want someone to make nice records, hire me a secretary. I'm giving people their share of American industry and I'm a believer. You better believe I'm a believer."

"Calm down, Roz," I told her. "We love you."

That was the only word that could work with her. I'm sure Odd Job hadn't said "love" since he told her years ago that he sure would love to know how her grandfather started in the supermarket business.

Ruthless Roz, despite the Depression of 1970, has grossed $40,000 the first six months of the year. The partner has ordered me to lay off and to continue handling her problems or she might move to another firm. I'm thinking of hiring a billboard myself.

Sonny Huber is most likely the kind of stockbroker you do business with. He is one of the thousands of people who entered the industry in the 1960's with one of two qualifications: either they were businessmen who had sold their businesses, had contacts and nothing else to do. Or they were sons who considered themselves rebellious, that is, they would not go into the slot all arranged for them in the family fur store. They would be eased into brokerage firms to accept commissions that the family could generate. (Some of these kids could make $20,000 to $30,000 a year on family-generated commissions alone and not get in anyone's way in the mink and Alaskan seal departments at the store. All they needed as brokers was to be able to distinguish between buy and sell.)

Sonny Huber had been a butcher, with a retail market that he shared with his first cousin. They sold to schools, restaurants, and country clubs, and each took a healthy living out of the business, not to mention an occasional lamb chop or prime rib. When urban renewal threatened to move a highway through their freezing compartments, Sonny and his first cousin closed their doors and retired. Each of them had upwards of $150,000 in cash, sitting deep in the ground in safe-deposit boxes.

After seven months of playing golf and gin rummy, however, Sonny decided he was too young to retire. People liked Sonny. He knew he would be a natural for the investment business. If he could sell meat, he could sell stocks. His first year in the market — 1968 — Sonny made himself $27,000 and he hadn't touched a dime from his safe-deposit box. In 1969, Sonny stumbled onto a theory:

he could make much more money for his customers and himself by purchasing only over-the-counter stocks in emerging companies — "concept stocks," in franchising, nursing homes, and pollution control. In January, February, and March of 1969, he was phenomenal. Often he was the only broker buying some of these issues, and his clients' orders competed with one another, forcing up thinly capitalized stocks 2 and 3 points with his own purchases. In June of 1969 his issues began to drop. But Sonny urged his clients to sit tight. "The concepts are still good," he said. The concepts may have been right, but Sonny hadn't been in the business long enough to learn to take small losses. When he was a butcher, the price of steak went only one way in twenty years — up.

The first six months of 1970, Sonny has earned $2,800, and only $120,000 of his cash is left, which he rushed into American Tel and Tel 8¾ debentures when they were offered. Wiping his hands on an imaginary apron he said, "The country is going to hell. But if A T and T goes down the drain, then *nothing* will have any value."

I have clients who said that, in the Bull markets of 1967 when Telephone was 62, in 1968 when it was 58, in 1969 when it was 51, now when it's 42. Sonny is thinking like a butcher, which is what his clients have been calling him ever since last July. He ate a piece of chicken from a drive-in restaurant franchised by one of his own over-the-counter companies. He got salmonellosis and is thinking of initiating a derivative stockholder suit.

"Lots of luck," his lawyer tells him, "the stock is *ten cents* bid. You put *me* in at $12. I'm the one who should sue *you*." Sonny is afraid to visit his nursing homes.

Everyone called Richard "Dickie," because that's what Dickie's father, George, called him. Dickie was a Big Producer for us and had a private office (two partitions), but he was removed from the center of the boardroom and the journeyman brokers who shared quotation machines and confidences. Unlike Sonny, who had been in business for himself, Dickie became a broker because his father was one of the biggest stock traders in the city; he never bought fewer than 1,000 shares. George had his own chair and phone in Dickie's office, the chair a modified executive swivel that the firm paid for. (It was the least we could do. Dickie's father in 1968 alone generated gross commissions of over $45,000, not to mention the bird-dogging he did for his son.) When we remodeled the office three years ago George helped pick the draperies.

"Money talks," the partner said to me later, going along with Dickie's dad.

George had sold a successful coat business to a Big Board textile manufacturer in 1958 and somehow discovered Syntex early, riding it from 2 to 130 and making the score of a lifetime — on paper. He had told all of his friends about it, long before the majority of Wall Street houses discovered it and bulled the stock. George rode Syntex up and down and pressured his son into the brokerage business and bullied his friends and former business associates to trade with Dickie. George by this time had become so famous for Syntex that everyone began referring to him as Georgie the Pill.

At the time Dickie became registered as a stockbroker, trainees still took the qualifying exam in their own firm's offices. (Now it is administered at independent sites). The entire accounting section of the exam was done for Dickie by an elderly broker who could read a balance sheet, while Dickie pored over the newspaper, underlining in red pencil his favorites that day at Aqueduct.

"We're not paying trainees for six months to flunk the registration exam," the senior partner told his branch offices. "They *will* pass," he added, never having gotten over the fact that he was a destroyer man in World War II. Wall Street abounds with destroyer men on the partnership level, all with framed photographs of their ships on their office walls. Whenever I see the senior partner of our firm I see Henry Fonda playing him, lobbing depth charges over the side.

Dickie passed the exam. His first day as a legitimate stockbroker George bought $100,000 worth of a mutual fund to put Dickie at the top of an office contest that was currently running. Salesmen who sold $75,000 worth of a particular fund within the contest's time limit (two months) won a trip to San Juan for a four-day sales conference. "It would be cheaper to send the kid without buying the stuff," said Georgie the Pill. "But that would be breaking the rules." There are reduced sales charges for large purchases of funds and George paid a load or commission of 3 per cent on his order. The next week, with the market up, Daddy sold the fund at a small loss, no commission charge. "Get the kid sales-oriented," said George. Dickie earned $1,000 (his share of the load) plus four business days in San Juan, where he skipped the conferences, spending his time sipping Piña Coladas at the bar and sleeping on a rubber raft in the middle of the pool of the Condado Beach Hotel.

Because Georgie the Pill made fortunes for people by recommending Syntex, his opinion was listened to on almost any other subject. His stock market tips became legendary because they were given by "the man who found Syntex at · two." Georgie the Pill would only pass on information to people who would buy from Dickie, and for a while Dickie was one of the biggest brokers in the city. But Georgie averaged Syntex all the way up, thinking it was going to 1,000. He also rode it all the way down, believing in its recovery, saying prayers for it at night. None of his friends knew that he hadn't sold and they kept believing in his touch, buying from Dickie until he buried them in National Video at 72 (now ten cents); McDonnell Aircraft at 50 (now 17) and Struthers Wells at 22 (now 4). Then he told everyone that Struthers had discovered a cure for baldness. When the customers complained to Georgie about being buried by Georgie's tips and Dickie's executions, Georgie said, "Don't bother me. I've got my own cancers. The market is a two-way street. They go down much faster than they go up. You got to know when to sell." He hit the complainers with twenty-two rapid-fire clichés and hung up on them.

Dickie now doesn't answer any calls he thinks may be complaints. He leaves a message that he'll call them back and he intends to. He just doesn't seem to get around to it. Georgie wishes he had never sold out to that textile company because our firm has taken away his desk and phone and his swivel chair. He now sits in a seat in front of the boardroom and prays for Syntex to recover. He's even taken some of the pills himself to find out if there are indeed any side effects. Dickie's production is running in the vicinity of $1,200 gross a month, mostly liquidation of accounts for margin calls, and his father doesn't even give him money for parking and tolls.

"Get me a chopped-liver sandwich, Dickie, will you," his father asked him the other day at lunchtime.

Dickie tensed all the muscles in his face and said, "It's Richard. For God's sake, Dad, it's *Richard!*" One of George's twenty-two clichés is that this Bear market will separate the men from the boys.

I've got to say a word about an efficient brokerage operation: our husband-and-wife team, Robert and Rebecca. Robert was a retired businessman who had a large portfolio and got tired of giving away commissions when he could earn them himself. In good markets, this kind of broker is trouble-free: pays for himself; takes up little space; makes no demands, and because he has few clients, has very few problems. Robert and Rebecca's children were all married and had moved away. Because of this, Rebecca developed the habit of coming into the office, taking Robert's letters and dialing his phone calls. Both of them were five feet four, white-haired, and organized to a degree that would have warmed the heart of Eugene Debs. Our resident partner believed that wherever possible he should bestow titles upon his personnel. I had taken a multiple-choice exam with one patriotic essay to become a manager. But the partner appointed Robert sales director. Rebecca bought him some desk display plaques — one with his name and, in bold letters, SALES MANAGER; another proclaiming SILENCE . . . GENIUS AT WORK. Robert's sales exhortations consisted of passing out the firm's research material, which flooded in on us weekly. "Stay on the phones," he reminded us. "Stay on the phones. You've got to move the goods. If it wasn't good the firm wouldn't push it. So push it."

No one paid much attention to Robert. After he distributed the flyers he'd waddle back to his desk and sit down next to Rebecca, who'd be busy dialing his next call. Their legs dangled over the edges of their chairs, their feet wiggling in space, not touching the floor. During a typical day Rebecca would call for Robert their druggist, their dry cleaner ("cleaners make a fortune; don't kid yourself"), their shoe repairman, and half the members of Robert's Blue Lodge (he was a Mason).

If the firm had recommended Detroit Edison at 17¾ he'd serve it up as if it were cherries jubilee. "They got the auto industry in Detroit, right?" he'd say. "You know how much power it takes to keep the factories open on double shifts?" Then, if it was a call to a home, Rebecca would ask to talk to the wife. "By the way," she would end her conversation, "you'll never get a bum steer from Robert. Let me put him on."

Because Robert recommends only conservative issues, his customers have made out better than most. They're not *making* money, but they've avoided disaster. But there is no public business today, and Robert's income has declined to the point where he and Rebecca account for almost half of his business trading their own money. They buy stock on the day before a dividend is declared, then sell when they're assured of getting it. Most of the time the commissions and the dividends came close to equaling the loss. We've demonstrated the madness in this method to them, but they look sadly down at their dangling feet and we feel sorry for them. When we turn away, the partner and I, Rebecca dials a number and Robert readies his presentation for the cleaner, the druggist or a fellow Hiram from the Lodge.

"Selling," he'd start. "I'm not selling anything. I'm doing you a favor . . ."

Clerical people are largely ignored in studies of the stock market, but they are tremendously important if you're choosing a broker or brokerage house to assist you. Very often, the order clerk, telegrapher, trader, or margin man can mean the difference between a well-executed order and a casual effort that may lose you (although you'll never know it) both time and money.

My boy Benjy has been studying for the registered representative's exam for thirteen years, but is never quite ready to go through with it. He is in charge of desk operations on all orders; the Telequote units, including the Trans-Jet price ticket; the air-conditioning controls; and the calendar for vacations and holidays. He is paid $139 a week, is at war constantly with the female secretaries and his female assistant, is forty-two years old and single, lives by himself in a rented room and is utterly loyal and conscientious.

Benjy almost married once, to a girl he met at an Over-Forty Mixer. It went as far as a ring selection, a dress for her, and, on the advice of a doctor, a circumcision for him. The dress and ring were returned, much to Benjy's relief, when he found out, just in time, that she planned to quit her job after the wedding. But it was too late to undo Benjy's operation.

Benjy was the fastest telegrapher in our system, the best over-the-counter trader, the quickest changer of tapes on the old Trans-Lux machines which used to transmit prices to us on the American and the Big Board. He hated and resisted every sign of mechanical progress in the industry, feeling that increased automation, along with female help, constantly threatened his status. "You-Mac bird," he'd yell at the secretaries when they'd come in after playing sick for a day.*

"You-Mac bird," he'd yell at a broker who entered a buy order when he meant sell and Benjy had to straighten it out.

"You-Mac bird," he'd type on the Teletype when messages from the enemy (the main office) came up that he didn't like.

"Benjy," I told him this morning, "we didn't have Memorial Day off because business is so lousy. I'm sorry to tell you that Columbus Day and Election Day and Armistice Day *and* Good Friday, we'll be working also."

"You-Mac bird," Benjy said to me, and I retreated to my office. You can put up with a lot of abuse from a loyal, conscientious, efficient, older man who arrives in snowstorms to run the machines for $139 a week.

And after all, our group insurance paid for half his circumcision.

---

*The You-Mac bird is an old joke which Benjy loved:
Question: What is the cry of the You-Mac bird?
Answer: F——k you, Mac . . .

3.

The Four-Seasons Syndrome

Monday, June 8:

I went through eight hundred customer statements over the weekend and I'm astonished at how much money has been lost. Not astonished. Sick. What it means is that the public, the average person with a few thousand dollars invested, is Rinso. Cleaned out. A stockbroker without institutional business or without money that he handles on a discretionary basis will be drawing the minimum wage ($277 a month). Because the "public" are the last people to get the word about improving conditions and buying opportunities.

These public people are often referred to with disdain as the "odd lotters." Even by brokers who handle *only* odd-lotters. No one likes to admit he is small potatoes, which is why so many people buy 100 or 200 shares of cheap mining and oil stocks when they should be buying 10 shares of Woolworth or 7 shares of American Home Products. But to casually mention over a leg of lamb special with mint jelly at the company cafeteria that you picked up a few hundred Aroused Porcupine Mines at 2½ — that's class, because that's a "round lot."

"Odd lots" are any purchase of stock under 100 shares. Each day the *Wall Street Journal,* on the next-to-last page, publishes how many shares in total the odd-lotters *bought* the day before and how many shares they *sold.* If they (the odd-lotters) keep selling more than they buy for a period of time, many Wall Street veterans say, "The market has got to go up; the odd-lotters are selling, on balance. They're always wrong; the small person has got to be wrong." This, and a certainty that the reverse is true, is the basis of the Odd-Lot Theory. Those poor small people: if they only knew how many big buyers, of thousands of shares, chase rumors and sell on bad news and buy on good news and lose money year in and year out, they might find some comfort. But probably not.

The Broadway producer who has a tremendous hit and establishes a major reputation is depressed. "What's the matter?" he is asked.

"It's not enough that I'm a tremendous success," he answers. "My best friend has also got to go broke." The stock market has the same history and most of the people who play it act exactly the same. I call them the "square-lotters." They play their games as they live their lives.

One of my odd-lotters called to switch 25 shares of

American Cyanamid into 25 shares of Fruehauf but what he really wanted was to complain. "For crying bells," he demanded, "all I hear about is *they* did that. *They* say this. *They* agree the market is poised to retreat to 500. Who the hell is *they*?"

A good question, and a lot of people ask it. Everybody talks about *they*, but nobody ever does anything about them. *They* actually possess all the secret wisdom of Wall Street and dictate the price movements and the reasons that stocks go up and down at given times. *They* actually are *everybody* with the exception of *you*. No matter who *you* are, you can never be *they*. Because *they* must exist in nameless limbo; a place of wisdom like Billy Batson's cave. And if I ever catch *they*, I'm going to punch him in the mouth.

The beginning of this week reminded me of the summer of 1960 when I was training in New York. No one could find anything for me to do so they'd give me three-page research reports and the first automatic stapler I had ever seen, with instructions to "collate this material." I knew from the army what collate meant, so I neatly stacked the pages and assembled them for hours until I could leave at four, grab a cup of Manhattan clam chowder and hope to meet young secretaries on the IRT. I was a hard hat in a three-piece suit.

Thursday, June 11:

I was awakened by a radio "morning man." "I asked my broker how much I'm worth," the announcer was saying. "And my broker said that the total can buy you a transfer to the unemployment line."

Full of optimism, I drove into town, blasting through a thirty-five-cent exact-change toll booth without paying and hearing the *annnh, annnh,* of the violation buzzer in back of me. When there's a long line and I don't have the change, I often do this, making it up sometime later by depositing seventy cents in the same thirty-five-cent box, just to let them know that stockbrokers can be honest even dealing with machines.

The partner greeted me, wiping perspiration from his brow. He couldn't wait to tell me that he had not slept in the last week. "Did you know?" he told me, "that one of the biggest houses on the Street was about to send eighteen hundred sell-out telegrams to customers on June 2. But delayed them when the market rallied."

Well, I already knew this, of course, but it was still serious because if other brokerage firms had the same situation, where customers' accounts were to be dumped, the mushrooming effect could produce panic. With all sellers and no buyers and a run to preserve *anything* out of an account, the major function of a stock exchange as a central marketplace could be eliminated. At which point the revolutionaries could use old IBM certificates with which to roll their joints.

Let me explain these "sell-out" messages. If a customer's equity in a margin account drops to below 35 per cent, we send out letters, or margin calls, asking for a deposit to bring the account back up to the required level. If no deposit is made after this request, brokerage houses then resort to the "sell-out telegram," usually delivered early in the morning or late at night to terrify the recipient. This imperative missive says something like THANK YOU FOR YOUR VALUED BUSINESS. UNLESS WE RECEIVE $175 BY 1 PM TOMORROW, WE RESERVE THE RIGHT TO LIQUIDATE ENOUGH SECURITIES FROM YOUR ACCOUNT TO COMPLY WITH MINIMUM NEW YORK STOCK EXCHANGE REQUIREMENTS. At the end of May, a former active trading account of mine whose portfolio had dwindled from some $40,000 to $6,000 got one of those telegrams, for $227. He called me at 9:01 in the morning. "You know what those idiots at your firm have done?" he screamed at me. "You know that for two hundred twenty-seven stinking dollars you're going to lose my account? Tell them that."

"We're a regulated business," I told him. "We have no control over the regulations."

"Well, I *have* control over my account and it's going to Merrill Lynch. And if *one* share of my stock is sold, I'll have the SEC all over you like a tent. My wife was hysterical over that telegram. She thought her mother had died."

"Uhhh. You going to send in the $227?"

"I gave your miserable firm $3,300 in commissions last year," he said.

"I gave you National Realty last year," I said. (National Realty then went from 12½ to 24).

"What'd you do for me lately?" he said and hung up.

I knew that he'd send in the money, but Western Union had snapped the delicate balance that a customer's man has these days with his customers. I called my margin department (the official section which regulates and figures clients' accounts and is responsible for ordering sell-out notices) to find out what could be done about midnight dunning messages. I got the margin clerk who handles our branch office and told him my problem. "I don't care who he is or what his account *used* to be worth," I was told. "His equity drops below 35 per cent, we send him a notice. He doesn't pay, we send him a telegram. We don't get the dough, we sell him out. Don't cry to me about the rules; I got my own problems."

But one of the many problems on Wall Street for the last five years was that everyone was too busy writing orders to bother about controls or courtesy. For a service-based industry where this very service was all we offer, it was too often sadly lacking. With overtime pay in 1967 and 1968, margin clerks were commanding $350 to $500 a week and were more pampered and pandered to than $200,000 no-cut rookies. They are now back to a normal $140 to $185 a week but generally could not give less of a damn about the complaints of the customers *or* the registered representatives. Working in New York had a lot to do with that. Many back-office personnel on Wall Street labored long hours at impossible tasks in crowded, noisy surroundings and dragged themselves home in fatigued condition without the benefit of even a bar car. In many cases it turned them into short-tempered, nasty people (especially to non–New Yorkers) who complained often and cursed the inefficiency of the system.

But no union has cracked them yet. Oh no! They have group insurance and profit sharing and they're capitalists.

But group insurance often means that you're covered for everything *except* what happens to you, and profit sharing only applies when companies and industries show profits. Upton Sinclair, where was you when we needed you?

Friday, June 12:

One of the leading financial columnists of our city said today that "those who say this is another 1929 don't know what they're talking about. More shirts were lost this time in a single month than in the whole 1929–1932 tragedy." Why do they have to keep reminding me, I thought, and forced myself to go into the office.

My first phone call depressed me further because if I had gotten it a year ago it would have made me jubilant. A client of mine had sold his well-run and profitable company to an over-the-counter conglomerate two years ago when the conglomerate was selling at $70 a share. My client got 200,000 shares of stock, a paper value of *$14 million.* He was blinded by what I call the "Four-Seasons Syndrome." All that my client had known or *knew* about or cared about for thirty years was manufacturing small fire extinguishers and alarm equipment. He made some of the best home disaster prevention devices in the country; made a profit for twenty-five years, and his idea of a big time was a $2 Nassau with automatic presses and winners-buy-the-drinks. One sad day in 1967 (sad for my client), a professional Deal Maker, a "finder," was driving his leased Continental from Boston to New York. He was driving partly because he feared airline shuttle service where no drinks were served, and partly so that as he noticed interesting company signs on interesting factories he could pull off the road and into the company parking lot and go in to see the president of the company and ask him if he was interested in selling out. If the finder, after a fast talk and display of his credentials, got an interested response, he would go off to New York and work on finding a buyer for the company by the side of the road.

The finder's fee would be adjusted according to a sliding scale — usually 5 per cent of the first million dollars, 4 per cent of the second million, 3 per cent of the third, et cetera. Pretty healthy for introducing a few people, and possibly getting away with rape.

One such "Freddie the Finder" found my client in just this way, setting him up with a New Jersey–based public company who was looking for a few solid businesses to dress up their earnings. The conglomerate flew my client into the Big Apple in their company Beechcraft, apologizing that it wasn't a Lear Jet. "We're solid people," they assured him, "with solid reputations. With the balance sheet we're trying to build, we don't have time for frills."

But a few of these trips — a few Casa Brasil Beef Wellingtons, a few strawberries Grand Marnier at La Grenouille, and other delights at the Sherry Netherlands, not to mention the promise of 14 million big ones — and all the $2 Nassau victories in the world could not keep him away. Now the stock my client holds is selling at 5. He has not sold a share (he cannot — he owns restricted, or "lettered," stock) and he no longer owns his own profitable company, which afforded him a handsome living for so many years. The conglomerate's last report to the stock-holders, for six months, showed a three-quarter-of-a-million-dollar loss. My client now knows the meaning of the Four-Seasons Syndrome.

I must say that the SEC is not *all* bad, even though their ranks are loaded with witch-hunters who combine the worst combinations of Napoleonic complex with student manager-of-the-football-team longings. In the matter of restricted, or "lettered" stock they really do protect the public. The SEC demands that insiders (corporate officials, finders, venture-capital people, and individuals receiving large amounts of stock in exchange for their companies or their services) be subject to long-term holdings for *investment purposes*. They must get an SEC letter of approval to register their stock for sale to another party *or* the public. If this rule did not exist, my client, the fire extinguisher manufacturer, presumably could have dumped his 200,000 shares on the market in the 70's and in the 60's (if there had been buyers) and bought his own fleet of Beechcrafts or even a few Phantom jets. Having this restricted stock has considerably limited the number of *real* millionaires in the last five years, as well as limiting rampant fraud in the marketplaces. On the other hand, such a concentration of stock has produced one phase of the current "liquidity crisis." Which is why my sadder but wiser client called in the first place.

"Got a problem," he said.

I said nothing, and he went on. "Two years ago I made a pledge to charity — $125,000 — and they are looking for their money. What kind of a price can you get me for

40,000 shares of my stock?" (Part of his holdings were now free, and registered for sale, on a sliding basis — so much each year could now be distributed to buyers in the open market.)

I told him I'd call back, and checked the pink sheets — the quotation service provided daily for every over-the-counter stock. Listed opposite the name of the security on this pink sheet are the dealers who carry inventories in the stock and the approximate prices (the bid and asked) at which each dealer *may* do business. There were six dealers in my client's company and I checked them all, getting a feel for the market. I didn't have to get a feel; I knew already what the answer would be. I could have sold approximately 1,000 of the 40,000 shares at *five* without disturbing the price. Perhaps another thousand at 4½, another at 4, and then — no more bids. I called my customer back. "If you'll settle for $10,000," I told him, "I think we can do business."

"What do you mean?"

"I mean that your order, in a depressed market, would drive the price of your stock to zero."

"I think I'm going to be sick," my client said, after a long pause. "What will I tell the charity? I made a pledge."

I didn't tell him that what he should do is ask the charity to put him on their list of needy cases. No dormitories will have *his* name on them this year.

This is "liquidity" in a marketing sense. You cannot sell *or* buy large amounts of stock now without violently affecting the price. A nimble broker could hit all six over-the-counter dealers simultaneously and sell each of them *some* stock before the others discovered the size of the order. But these days they'll only take 100 or 200 shares per phone call. And next time you ring them, they'll stick it in your ear. Over-the-counter dealers have died with their inventories. They're stuck at higher prices with merchandise that is now depressed. And they've got little or no chance of selling it to anyone.

The biggest money in Bull markets of the last ten years has been made over-the-counter. Because the swings in prices can be so violent; because in most cases you're trading blind; and because no one has time to check a story or a tip. If you don't buy immediately and check later, the stock might be 30 per cent higher. Many mutual funds operated on this theory in 1966–1969. I ran into a college friend at drinks a few weeks ago. He helped run a portfolio of $20 million for a medium-sized growth fund with a great reputation in the late 1960's. Juniper Berry, they used to call him in college, because of the amounts of gin he consumed.

"Hi, Junie," I said. He had done me some favors over the years, once calling me after a four martini lunch to throw me 3,000 Sears, Roebuck to sell for his fund. It was like handing me a $600 present. The next day he called again. It seemed he was staying in town. Did I know any TWA stewardesses who were sure things for a client and himself?

The closest I got to his fund's business after that *and* to Sears, Roebuck was when I opened a charge account to buy a power lawnmower.

But when I saw Junie this time, during an extended trip through a bottle of Tanqueray, he told me that he was "at liberty" and interviewing other funds and money managers. He had been let go for "lack of performance" in the past fifteen months. And he was bitter. "If the public knew what went on," he said, "we'd have been bombed and stormed by crowds. They sent me out last March, for instance, to look at a company over-the-counter, manufacturing components for Community Antenna Television. Okay, it's selling at 17 and I visit them and find out they can't pay their bills; their chief engineer has just quit to go with RCA; the president is getting a divorce and cannot function; and they've never made a nickel but had repeatedly predicted turning the corner next year. They were going to turn the corner, all right. Only they were turning it further into the red. I cannot *believe* this company, okay? Even though they had a very glamorous name. I make my report to the investment committee at the fund that we avoid the situation. *Then* I find out we *already* bought 30,000 shares between 12½ and 16 without ever *giving them a phone call.* We heard Fidelity and Enterprise were buyers and we couldn't wait, I was told. When the stock was 7, shortly thereafter, we swallowed and sold our block at 4. As it happened, Fidelity and Enterprise never did buy any. Want another cute story?" Junie said.

I nodded.

"Okay," he said. "We manage money, right? We had managed accounts, for people with a minimum of $100,000. They give us the money and we run it, like a trust department at a bank. Only with some action. Well,

switches in the management personnel took place constantly and some portfolios were in stocks that went bank-
rupt — went to twenty-five or thirty *cents. Cents. Before*
we discovered that we had customers in those stocks. Gross
negligence! People with $100,000. And no one will ever
really know the story."

"I'll have another one of these," he told the bartender,
"with five onions, please."

Monday, June 15:

The only cheery note is that bond yields are the highest
in history. A West Virginia college marketed a tax-free
municipal bond to raise $2,875,000, bearing a yield to the
buyer of almost 8½ per cent. *Tax-free.* For a man with
$1 million invested in these bonds, it would mean $85,000
a year with no federal taxes to pay. The new math can be
fun.

I have a new account this morning, a group of young
men who are running $2 million, garnered from some
wealthy produce men who have no time to run the money
themselves. (The produce men are at the market district
from three-thirty in the morning to seven at night and
never eat dinner because they're so full of sample bites of
avocados, grapefruits, melons and apples.) The manager
of this money sat opposite me, a bit suspicious that I
might be over thirty. He calls his group a hedge fund, but
he is conscious of only *one* direction on Wall Street —
down. He's twenty-three years old, wears bell-bottoms,
drives an Eldorado and lives at home with his parents.
"I'm Wild Bob the Bear," he said to me, "and I don't care."

It was refreshing to meet someone so positive about directions in the market. He went on, shaking his hair out of his eyes every few seconds. It was done in a pageboy, like Prince Valiant's. With the Dow-Jones at 685, Bob says "Fifty per cent of the companies over-the-counter and on the curb are going to Q, the financial page's footnote for bankruptcy. No one believed it. My generation will be able to buy all these companies for five to ten cents and reorganize them. This is a battlefield, man; you got to discipline yourself. Do you know that the Dow-Jones has, on average, only advanced 4.5 per cent a year since its beginnings? Four point five per cent. I could get that in a coma. Look, I'm a scientist, right?" (He had an engineering degree.) "Everything is thermodynamics, heat transfer, and it all boils down to equilibrium. The averages are going to 450."

I was nodding my head as fast as I could.

There are two kinds of customers in the brokerage business: those who can be helped, and those who are beyond it. But there is no doubt about our function as mere order takers. Buy 1,000 Ford; sell 500 Itek. That's easy. Bob the Bear didn't need or want advice; he just wanted a sounding board.

And he went on:

"The average consumer in the United States is two and a half years in debt on his salary. You got to go short, keep shorting, and stay short."

"Do I *ever* buy?" I asked him, watching his hair go flip-flop.

"The man with $10,000 at the bottom of his market will make a million dollars."

"What do I buy?" I asked.

"You buy IBM at 47."

"I've got $10,000," I thought, wildly excited. This kid had me thinking like a customer. It's a difficult business to maintain perspective in.

He got up. "I've got to go to the produce market," he said. "You'll be hearing from us. I like your style. If you want a little friendly tip, you short the secondary companies that live off the big ones. They're the ones that are going to Q." He gave me the V sign and ambled out.

I punched H & R Block on my quotation machine, the stock I had shorted at 47. It was 51 in a dreadful market and I quickly erased the price and symbol, hoping to erase it from my mind.

The average person never sells short. He refuses to understand the process of borrowing something he doesn't own to sell it, with the promise of giving it back sometime in the future. Despite the pessimism that is gripping the country, most people are optimistic in their wishful thinking, in their fantasies. They *want* to be successful; they *want* to be rich; they *want* peace and prosperity to exist. (And don't tell me about the younger generations. I had a revolutionary call me to find out about shorting Eastman Kodak, knowing a week before the planned event that an all-out assault on their Rochester operations was planned. I told him he needed a minimum of $2,000 in his account. He told me he had some fine hash and a carload of amphetamines in Trenton, and he got furious that I did not take him seriously. If we could get hippies to play the market the threat of youthful revolution would be removed.)

People want prosperity; this is why they buy a stock at 20, see it go to 5, and hold on. They're hoping it will come back. It's also why, if they sell a stock *short* at 20 and it goes to 22, they cannot stand the heat. They call to check the stock three times a day, and if it drops to 20½ they cover, tickled pink to almost break even. People find it difficult to hold a short position, because it's not only betting against the country, it's betting against themselves. Besides, if you carry a short, it can, presumably, go to 1,000, to 10,000, the wrong way. If it drops and you make a profit, you can only make 100 per cent on your money. "Nervous in the service," Jim Curran calls people who go short stocks. "It's against human nature," he'd say, and I have to agree with him. Especially in view of the fact that so many hedge funds have disappeared from the phone book in the last fifteen months.

Monday, June 22:

All you hear now is the *other* liquidity crisis, the enormous failure of the Penn Central, the company on the Big Board with the longest continuing dividend record. All the brokers are wondering about the possibilities of a major panic if Penn Central goes under. "God, they'll take the Chase Manhattan with them," said Roz the Ruthless.

"Do you think it'll affect Asamera?" said Donald Counts, worried about his patrimony.

The partner called me in for a chat, which he does frequently to have a sponge for his fears. He dare not pass these fears on to our customers. "This could be it," he tells me. "There is $39 *billion* in commercial paper outstanding in this country as of May. What if there's a run on this paper and the companies can't pay? You've heard of the domino effect? Well, because of Penn Central's bankruptcy proceedings, there is a doubt about *every* company with a major debt structure. There could be mass disaster, and we're closer to it than people think. Commercial paper was not a factor in 1929, and it's not federally regulated now. Why did I go to Wall Street?" he says. "I could be in a law firm. I could've gone to medical school and become a radiologist."

Sonny Huber, the ex-butcher, pokes his head in to say good morning. "I got no sympathy at home," he adds. "My wife thinks a depression means that she uses a caddy instead of a golf cart."

"Chrysler will be the next company in bankruptcy," the partner says. "What next, O Lord?" Church attendance may be up.

Penn Central opened today on 450,000 shares at 6½. A nice woman who owned the stock at 53 called me at noon to check on it. She was a widow but kept herself attractive, as these women often do. I always wondered why she called *me*, because her voice dripped with scepticism at everything I said. She took an investment course a year ago from a nice middle-aged broker whose firm hired him the Gay Paree Room at a local motel. The Gay Paree Room had murals of the Seine, a portable blackboard, a lectern and seventy-five unfolded bridge chairs. The broker had mentioned Penn Central in the 50's: "If the company were liquidated," he said, "with their property and real estate holdings alone the stock is worth $90 a share." She bought it. He mentioned Four-Seasons Nursing at 70. "There is enormous profit potential in care for the aged. I might even be needing one of the homes myself someday. Sooner than I think." The widow was filled with sympathy and bought the stock at 67. It's now 1.

"I know your mother and like her," she told me. "Don't try to give me advice. I need someone with a bit of maturity. I'll give you the orders; you try and get me cheap prices when we buy." Today she sounded as if she had shrunk twelve inches and wrapped an afghan around her shoulders. "The president of Penn Central really shouldn't be drawing $250,000 a year," she said, "do you think?"

I didn't think so.

"But their land holdings alone are worth $90 a share."

"Why don't you ask your old teacher what *he* thinks," I suggested.

"Oh, I could never call him," she said. "He's much too busy."

Yes, I thought, saying the prayer for the dead. I was pretty sure the old broker tried to get her upstairs from the Gay Paree Room. The SEC would love *that*.

It's interesting that the majority of investors never use their brokers properly. An award of $296,520 was made today by a San Francisco court to a widow whose account was churned disastrously in a period (1963–1967) when stock prices were generally showing the biggest increases in history. Her account declined in this period from $533,000 to $251,000, mostly the result of a constant turnover in her portfolio.

How can you tell if *you* are being "churned"? Basically, if your broker, after a while of dealing with him, tells you: "Look. I'm here all the time and you're there. Give me discretion over your account and we can make some *real* dollars. I mean *percentage* gains are very nice with 50 shares here, 100 shares there. But it's the *dollar* amount that should count." Anyone would see some logic in this, so the broker is given permission. To prove his wisdom, he buys 600 shares of something that goes up 2 points in a week. He sells and calls the client. "Twelve hundred dollars' profit in a week," he says. (He doesn't mention that the figure is less costs). "Multiply that out it's $4,800 a month, $57,600 a year."

"Where has this been all my life?" the client says.

But the next week the broker buys 1,000 shares of something that "doesn't work out quickly enough," and he dumps with a half-point loss. "Five hundred dollars," he says. But it's more like $800 or $900 after commissions. Then, there's the distinct possibility that he'll double up on something else to get even the next time. This is churning. Eventually it eats the client alive and generates almost as much money in commissions to the broker as the customer has sustained in losses.

Of course individual clients usually do a worse job on themselves churning than brokers can do. Except clients call it "short-term trading." Short term is defined as the holding period on a stock up to *six months* from purchase. But short-term traders seldom hold that long; two weeks to three months is the average. Then they get itchy and have to be on a new horse. I make my living basically from short-term traders, who do not care about holding the six months or more to qualify being taxed at a lower rate. The swingers open an account and say, "You're watching the tape all the time. It must be easy to pick off $100 or $200 a day, just buying something that's active."

Don't try it, is my advice. You've *got* to be a loser on a short-term basis in the market. Maybe not immediately. You might have three great months, eight great months, a great year. But then you give it all back. Because if you can make $8,000, $10,000, $25,000, trading one year, you think that you've got the system, and *next* year it'll be $100,000, a quarter of a million. Only *next* year is 1962, or 1966, or 1970. You've doubled up and it's craps.

Nobody, thank goodness, ever pays any attention and they go on, banging away, making 3, 4, 5 points, 10 points in some situations, losing 3, 4, 5 points or 15 points in others, hoping the losers will come back, and eventually selling them out on the bottom. Because traders can never stay around for the *long* ride, they end up losers. Believe me, you can not call your broker more than *once a day* and make money.

Knowing every fraction of a point change in his stock makes a holder nervous. Invariably this is what happens — from my file of true confessions. January 1966. I have all my traders in Control Data around 32. By March it's 28 and my traders are tired of holding; later in the year it's 24 and they're tired of their broker. They hear that Control Data is all finished; all the vice-presidents are leaving the ship (always a good time to buy). The stock struggles back and most of them break even, grateful to bail out. Others hold for 38, 39, and in January of 1967 it's 40. Everyone left in the stock runs like a thief, to go where the real action is. By the next fall, Control Data is pushing 160, the stock of the year, and *not one* trader owns it. If there are no atheists in foxholes, there are no *consistently* successful traders on Wall Street. I'd say that goes *double* for Main Street, except for the fact that the dumbest traders of all live in New York City.

Big Producers in brokerage offices usually change their largest accounts every year. Because of turnover and the pattern followed by most short-term traders, who move big money, trade big blocks, become burnt-out cases, and slink back after two or three years to buy "a little American Hospital Supply for the kids. Just buy it and put it away." They've become members of "TA" — Traders Anonymous!

Monday, June 29:

And all of our troops are out of Cambodia on schedule. The market closes at 682.91, down 4.93. During the day, President Nixon said that "the Middle East is now a bigger threat than Vietnam," and Jim Curran asks the brokers what the fastest thing alive is.

"Giraffes can do thirty-five mph," says Donald Counts.

"An ostrich," says Michael, my ex media rep.

Jim Curran shakes his head. "The fastest thing alive," he says, "is an Israeli paddling down the Suez Canal in a canoe."

"Why don't you guys make a few phone calls," I told them. "Buy *Polaroid* in the low 50's."

They grumble and pick up their phones, most of them to dial their wives. I'm on to their tricks.

4.

Research:
The Information Is from
Sources Considered Reliable

Tuesday, June 30:

A customer of mine runs an employment agency. He recently had a call from a Big Board company with much government business, who told him they were laying off nine hundred people, most of them with graduate degrees. "Can you place them?" he was asked.

"On a kibbutz in the Negev Desert," my client answered. He is always ready with a quip.

"But the joke," my client told me this morning, "the joke, Brutus. I think of you. You know, the prostitute walking on the sands at Miami Beach? She says she's selling, are you buying? And the businessman takes her up on her proposition, only to discover, when he gets back to New York, that it hurts when he goes to the bathroom.

"The next winter he goes to Miami Beach again and the same prostitute walks by. She says she's selling, 'Are you buying?' 'What are you selling this year?' asks the business-man. 'Cancer?' "

I know the feeling well. It's hurting *me* all the time, too.

A word about Florida, while we're on the subject. The state of Florida has ruined more investors than any Bear market in history. Why is this? Because thousands of in-vestors from the eastern United States go to Florida in the winter: a few weeks in Miami, a quick jaunt to Grand Bahama, a month in Palm Beach. Second homes and condominiums and a Place in the Sun.

I have three clients who are retired businessmen. "Con-sultants," they call themselves — with amusement, be-cause the term was not invented until after they retired. They play golf at the same country club in the summer-time, in a threesome at seven in the morning. They always lose a ball apiece on the first hole, duck-hooking into trees forty yards out. If it gets cold enough in the fall to play in sweaters, they take their wives and go south to Florida, knowing that winter is on its way. When they're not on the golf courses of Miami, they sit in brokerage boardrooms, listening to gossip, telling stories and trading.

The brokerage office has assumed the traditional role of a Roman bath or synagogue for thousands of older people in this country, and the stockbroker has become a priest or rabbi they can really communicate with. But whenever my clients return north in the spring, it takes months for them to recover from the disaster of Florida tips. Let me explain by setting a scene. Picture a Miami brokerage office on Collins Avenue in February with lots of chairs for customers because there are always lots of customers in Miami in February. The point is, there is very little loyalty to their brokers up north: customers always take the most comfortable, most convenient spot to do business. "The prices are all the same," my three clients tell me. "You can do without the business for a few months, a bright kid like you. We go where the beach is near and the company is good. Like a club. You understand."

"I understand," I tell them. "Just don't get yourselves loaded with junk."

But, like a mother warning her kids not to eat too many sweets, or reminding them not to put beans up their noses while she is out, it is no use. They wander into the plush boardrooms, take front seats, light up cigars made in Tampa by Cubans, and watch the ticker tapes. Someone sitting a few seats away tells them a story about Brunswick making a comeback.

"That's an *old* story," my clients respond, having each owned Brunswick in the past on similar comeback rumors.

"New things are happening," the stranger insists. "Look! There's 10,000 on the tape, insider buying. Fund buying. You don't see buying like that unless something's going on. I bought 1,000 myself. Last week." That usually does it. Being told by someone who makes a lot of noise that he recently bought 1,000 shares is sure to trigger a reaction.

"Buy me 100 Brunswick," says my first client to any nearby broker.

"Buy *me* 100 Brunswick," says my second client.

Another 3,000 shares go by on the tape, up a quarter of a point.

"Christ, it's moving away," says the stranger.

"Buy me 200 at the market," says my third client, getting excited.

My clients buy stocks in the morning, go to the pool or play golf, come in for lunch, sell stocks in the afternoon, play some gin rummy and retire to their rooms for pre-dinner naps. When they come north in the spring, they are tanned and sheepish. And they show me their portfolios, loaded with New Issues, over-the-counter dogs, and whatever the current listed favorites were in the Sunshine State. "Arthur Godfrey bought this one," I am told, about one oil stock on the American Exchange which has since been delisted and sells for eight cents.

"I *saw* Jackie Gleason walk in, buy 3,000 of this and pay for it in cash," they tell me. "A roll like a cucumber. All $100 bills."

Each of them naturally bought the same stock, hoping, I suppose, that some of the glitter would rub off and that *they* would someday be able to introduce the June Taylor Dancers.

When they were in Miami last winter my absentee clients bought companies importing jukeboxes that simultaneously played songs and showed films; companies that manufactured soft drinks in aerosol cans for burn patients; companies that promised to get lobsters off the continental shelf and companies that promised to squeeze all the abandoned autos in the country into pellets the size of marbles and distribute them as toys in underprivileged countries. We have sold all of the stocks at large losses, but the three customers never seem very sorry and they never learn their lesson. "We *had* to buy stock to sit in the offices down there. Where else had we to go? What else had we to do?

We can always get money. The companionship was good. What was so bad?"

There are several lessons to be learned from all this. First and foremost, if you are serious about your money, don't go to Florida boardrooms in the winter. I can see the figures now in our Miami office daily and they are running up to 80 per cent *behind* last year and the year before that, because most of the Florida retail brokerage activity has been generated in a helter-skelter grab for action. Capital gains, as in the case of my three clients, are a secondary consideration. This is most frustrating to a customer's man who believes in the system of making money for his clients. In a lot of cases it is *not* what the customer wants, and certainly not what he needs.

I'm sure it comes as no surprise to anyone who has dealt with the public to know that we fill as great an emotional need as a physician fills a physical need. And I'm not talking about fraud or dishonesty, I'm talking about some people's obsession with losing, about some people's need to have their money turn over, and about most people's need to belong. If the stock market is where the action is, that's where they are, big and small, from the Teamsters' pension fund to the Catholic Church to Apple Annie, who I'm sure would put a few dollars on Minnie Pearl Fried Chicken (now Performance Systems and down the drain) if the timing were right.

The one thing that makes stockbrokers so boring and customers so interesting is that brokers very seldom talk about anything but stocks, bonds, commodities, and the price of money. My three Florida-wintering clients could care less about stocks. What they care about is the past, very deeply, and they care about life. This is why, even beyond the pronouncements from the Board of Governors of the New York Stock Exchange, a central marketplace is needed. Not just to raise capital for companies in a capitalistic society, but to satisfy the insatiable requirements of the public's imagination.

Wednesday, July 1:

Forbes magazine, in their latest issue, says, "It would be foolish to underestimate the damage that has been done and how long it will take to undo it. A crash is a crash is a Crash."

The resident partner came into my office at the opening of the market and looked gray. "From nine o'clock to ten. Not *one* phone call," he said. He had the daily commission figures from each office in his hand, including figures on the $15 surcharge per trade on orders up to and including 1,000 shares. (This charge was instituted by the exchange on April 1 as an interim measure until the commission scale for the industry could be raised.) "Representative Moss from California wants this investigation of the surcharge extension which expires tomorrow," says the partner. "I'll leave the business if the extension is not granted. Moss wants the public record in this regard." Moss is trying to protect the small investor, who presumably is hurt most by the surcharge and by the proposed commission rate increases, which would raise rates by 50 per cent on trades up to $5,000.

"A rolling stone," I said, but he paid no attention.

"Public record, for God's sake," he went on. "We lost a

million dollars last month and they're pussyfooting around. With the country coming down around our ears."

The partner went on. "The trouble with this industry is that it's probably too damned honest. Dumb but honest. All our prices are public. Everyone sees the commissions on their confirmation slips. You buy a trunk for galoshes from a decorator for $200. *He* paid $7.50, polished the brass handles and slapped some varnish on it. You take your car in to be tuned and they loosen two things for every one thing they tighten and you don't drive out for under $100. Ever. It must be an industry minimum. If the surcharge is not extended, I'm not only leaving the business, I'm assassinating Representative Moss."

People like to tell stockbrokers their troubles, and on these 8-million-share days there is plenty of time to chat. We are all prisoners in the same concentration camp. There are no heroes anymore, only horror stories. "Eight million shares," you say. "Why that's double what the volume was in the fifties and early sixties. Surely there is trading somewhere."

Let me put the volume situation to rest for you people who do not haunt boardrooms. Eight million shares today is like 3 million in 1961–1962, because the number of shares outstanding has increased nearly fivefold, the number of companies on the Big Board has practically doubled, and the number of stockbrokers has increased dramatically. Thus, if every broker did enough business on a given day to buy himself a cup of coffee and a grilled cheese sandwich, the Big Board would trade 7.5 million shares. And nothing left over for rent, groceries, or the installment on their BankAmericard. (This is, of course, an oversimplification to let you know that on an 8- or 9-million share day, institutions might account for 30 to 40 per cent, floor trading for another healthy slice, the rest scattered among offices from Odessa, Texas, to Madrid, Spain. So 85 per cent of all stockbrokers are feeling their palms sweat and their stomachs ache from Fear. There will be a lot of divorces if we continue having 8-million-share days.)

I take the time on a day like today to have my salesmen come in, one by one, for a little heart-to-heart. To find out if there is any way I can breathe some life into their sagging enthusiasm for the business.

Leslie Lewis came in to see me with a hopeless smile on his face. He thought he was about to be fired and smiled to show that he didn't care. "The boy stood on the burning deck," he said.

Leslie is a man, a young broker in his mid-twenties who trained in New York and wanted to come to this city to live and practice his chosen profession. You cannot make it cold in this city with just brains and a handsome face. Knowing no one in town when he arrived, Leslie called on doctors from the yellow pages, lawyers from the yellow pages, and customers in our dead files who had done business with us over the years, who had used brokers either no longer in the market or now working for other firms. When a broker leaves a firm's employ, his customers are immediately divided among the survivors in the office and immediately contacted to retain them for the firm if possible. It's picking the bones before the corpse is cold, and many people resent it, but as Bluebeard used to say, life goes on. Ships that pass in the night.

71

If you are choosing a stockbroker, choose one who is successful and who seems to have no free time. A hungry broker will press for business. Without actually being dishonest, he may nevertheless make decisions that he suspects may not be suitable for the customer — just to make that commission. Leslie had two transactions in the last month that were reneged on by customers who claimed they never ordered the stock. Leslie swore they had given him the orders. This occurs when you make cold calls in a strange city or when you reactivate the dead file.

"You want to know about my aunt," said Leslie. "What can I say? She likes action."

I looked at him. Leslie's aunt lived in Fort Lauderdale and sent him $5,000. Her instructions were to double it, but not to take any risks. Leslie churned his aunt unmercifully, taking small losses and small profits. The commissions ate up $700 over a three-month period. "I'm afraid you're going to have to redouble your finger-walking through the yellow pages," I told him. "Put your aunt in American Sterilizer at 13 and call it a day."

"Let's face it," he told me. "I was a stranger in the city, out of town were the people I knew . . ." Leslie was really a very likable guy.

"You're in the wrong business," I told him. "In the wrong town, in the wrong era."

"To be honest with you," he said, "I'm moonlighting as a bartender in a dating bar. And it might become full time. This is getting to be a sick joke. You think I like churning my aunt? Despite the fact that she deserves it?"

"Stay on through the summer," I told him. "Maybe we'll have a turnaround."

I didn't believe a turnaround would help Leslie and neither did he. He was about to leave my office when he said, "I feel like Stella Dallas. The world is passing me by."

Sonny Huber, the ex-butcher, came in loaded with facts about little-known things. He believed without question everything he saw in newspapers, in magazines, and on television. "I heard," he said, "that the IRS center (the one serving New York and New England) has already paid *$2 billion* in refunds this year. The government is going broke. How can I sell stocks with any conviction when I don't believe in them myself?"

"How's your money holding out, speaking of the IRS?" I asked him.

"Christ. I've been advised to put the rest into Swiss francs or German marks. Anything to get it out of this country. How's the weather in Switzerland in July?"

There isn't much point arguing with an irrational man, but I told Sonny at least to call people about utility stocks, many selling at ten-year lows and carrying record-high yields. Safety. A refuge.

"Are you kidding?" Sonny said, "when the utilities have to borrow money at 10 per cent? They'll all go to hell. Did you know that the Chilean escudo is being devalued for the eleventh time *this year*?"

"I think you're in the wrong business."

"I think we're *all* in the wrong business," Sonny snapped back.

I tried to get Donald Counts off the subject of Asamera Oil long enough to urge him to develop some commodity customers. Commodities (wheat, soybeans, pork bellies, corn, silver, etc.) can give you the ride of your life — quickly and painfully. Study them if you wish by reading the reams of material printed daily about rainfall, crops, prices, metals, droughts, floods, wars, typhoons — all those common everyday occurrences that affect commodities — and you will emerge as mystified as you were before you began. I have *never* seen an individual trader, a nonprofessional, in commodities who did not go broke. Futures trading is fine if you are in a commodity-oriented business — if you're a farmer, rubber grower, baker, or Mr. Hershey from Hershey, Pennsylvania — as a hedge against your inventories. But for Mr. Action with $2,000 in his fist, it'll be a fast two or three passes and — tap city. I won't dwell on the subject, because nobody, be he chartist or student of grain cycles, knows a damn thing about commodities. It's a crap shot at best. But unfortunately, these days on Wall Street, it may be the only game in town.

"I lost $1,500 on three Rapeseed contracts once," Donald Counts told me. "My father bought the contracts on a tip. He was intrigued by the name. Then he bought sugar in 1959 when Castro was taking over Cuba. I think sugar was up the limit for three days in a row. Dad made a killing, then gave it back in hides the next year. He's never gotten a good story from anyone in the shoe business. They're always wrong."

Remembering his sugar success, Donald launched into stories of the good old days in Havana, when men were men and women were five American dollars. "I spent weeks at a time in Havana," he told me, "going every day to see Superman, the man with the world's largest organ. Sometimes he'd perform with three girls; sometimes with married women from the States. Volunteers from the audience. There was nothing like Havana in the good old days."

"Maybe," I suggested, "maybe you can get your father interested in some Rapeseed again."

It was gratifying to chat with Roz the Ruthless, who spent her moments with me complaining about her husband and how cheap he was becoming. "Can you believe," she told me, "that he buys his ties from our local cleaner for seventy-five cents apiece. Rayon and acetate ties that hang on a rack at the cleaners."

I told her that times would get better and her husband would once again be introduced to Countess Mara. Then I suggested she look at Cenco Instruments around 19½. It had been 63 a year ago.

"None of those government-contract companies," she said. "I can't *give* away an aerospace stock."

"Cenco works on optics," I told her. "The government probably won't cut out any of the areas Cenco is working on. The stock is cheap."

"I'll sell some," she said, and she went off to her phone, doing 400 shares before the end of a dull day. Her share of the commissions generated was enough to buy her husband fifty rayon and acetate ties.

Thursday, July 2:

I spent the next day in more therapeutic discussions with my salespeople, hearing about outrageous dentist's bills ($92 for two children in one day, with the dentist suggesting that my salesman use his Master Charge card to budget the payments.) The market was up 1.51 to 689.14, the worst *up* day I've seen in ten years. There were rumors of a bomb exploding on Wall Street. But on inspection it turned out to be only a firecracker.

Monday, July 6:

This morning we began with a unique American institution: the conference call from the home office's research department. We all sat around the middle of the boardroom and waited for the phone ring to activate our intercom-amplifier system. Everyone was supposed to be in at nine, to hear the recommendations from New York and be on the phones recommending the recommendations at nine-forty-five. At nine-ten, amazingly, everyone *was* in, except Dickie and his father, Georgie the Pill, who was never even *alive* before eleven.

At nine-fifteen we all had coffee, and the Teletype rattled a message to us which Benjy, the order clerk handed over. DUE TO A MALFUNCTION IN THE PHONE SYSTEMS, it said, THE CONFERENCE CALL WILL BE DELAYED UNTIL NINE-THIRTY. DO NOT LEAVE OFFICE. It was signed by the partner in charge of research, whose most notable accomplishments are that he owns one hundred and twenty-five pipes and that he constantly gets into automobile accidents, lost in his meditations about the perfect rail merger or the ideal takeover candidate. His clothes smell like a curing shed at P. Lorillard.

"Good morning, gentlemen and ladies," he began, when the system finally operated. "A few general comments at the outset. It is our belief that our system is here to stay —"

"Hear, hear," said Jim Curran, who got a dirty look from our resident partner, who was taking notes.

"— if I may borrow a phrase from a gentleman who helped to get us in this mess," the raspy transmission of the conference call went on, "the only thing we have to fear, is fear itself."

"Fear, fear," Curran whispered. But he could not be heard in turn by the apparatus, which worked only one way.

"We are surrounded, literally," the research partner went on, "by enemies from all sides, threatening our very existence as a central marketplace. Of course, our own company, although buffeted by the tides of change and a rotten market, remains strong, and, we hope, shortly will be able to resume the growth pattern of the past."

The brokers fidgeted in their seats, catching each other's eyes and trying to avoid mine.

"With the market under 700 and many historic lows facing us in the face, I want to say a few words about Chrysler (16¾) and the liquidity crisis."

The gist of the report was that our company felt that Chrysler could meet its debts, pay off its commercial paper-holders, and should be bought on a speculative basis "around these levels." Then, the research partner introduced two of our in-house analysts, who discussed and recommended Crowell-Collier (the encyclopedia kings) at 11 and three utilities — producers of natural gas, which evidently would be in short supply in 1971. It was easy for most of us to spew these stories back at the customers, especially stories about utilities, which would frighten no one. Buying Chrysler with such recent tremendous pressure on the stock, which obviously had come from institutional sellers, took some guts, and most investors that we called were not interested.

I bring up the conference-call sales meeting to give you an idea of how stocks are very often marketed. We as a firm have no vested interest in Chrysler or Crowell-Collier or any of the listed stocks we may recommend. What we care about is doing business. Merchandising is a major function of brokerage houses. Many firms run sales contests with monthly results posted in the offices, much like on the walls of your friendly local Chrysler dealer. As a matter of fact, we prefer our salesmen using our house research ideas rather than going off on their own tangents. At least the house can keep close watch on their own recommendations and not get sued for some stiff a salesman sells on his own.

One problem, however, is follow-up (in case you ever buy a stock on the basis of brokerage research.) I've recommended stocks over the years that appeared on our Monthly Buy List. Twentieth Century Fox was one, and I started accumulating it at 40. Someone was always looking to buy out Twentieth Century Fox at fancy prices or it was *rumored* someone was looking. A few months after my initial interest it was recommended again at 32; next month at 26, then at 19; then it suddenly disappeared from our list. The stock was 13. I wired our research department and asked why it had been removed.

OH, I was told, WE'VE LOST INTEREST IN THAT ONE. PROSPECTS FOR A TURNAROUND NEVER MATERIALIZED,

NOR DID A TAKEOVER. AND THE ANALYST WHO FOLLOWED THE COMPANY NO LONGER WORKS FOR US. WE RECOMMEND TAKING LOSSES.

WHERE DOES THAT LEAVE ME? I asked by wire.

No answer.

WHERE DOES THAT LEAVE ME, RE TWENTIETH CENTURY. 2ND REQUEST, I wired.

Two hours later came a brief reply. "RE TWENTIETH CENTURY FOX. REFER TO OUR INTEROFFICE MEMO OF MARCH 19. BELIEVE CAN BE SWITCHED INTO COLUMBIA PICTURES FOR PARTICIPATION IN LEISURE-TIME, ENTERTAINMENT FIELD."

"That was a wonderful suggestion," said a client when I apologized. (He had bought it at 40.) "What are you selling *this* year, cancer?"

Everyone had heard the joke.

There are a lot of pipe smokers in research departments on Wall Street, and a lot of stock analysts who switch their jobs with great rapidity. Why have this staff at all? Because stockbrokers are 90 per cent salespeople. They have no time nor talent for research on their own (other than flipping through a Standard and Poor's Stock Guide to give you last year's high and low prices). And salespeople need ideas; they need a crutch. On average, as I have said, they are the laziest class of people who go into an office to take up desk space.

A solution for this problem of nonprofessionals in a nonprofessional industry is *not* business schools and MBA's. Nor longer training programs (now an average of six months) as they now exist. Nor stiffer examinations.

The solution is to have *no* stockbroker allowed into the industry who has not worked *in business* for at least two years, so that every stockbroker *knows* what problems are posed in day-to-day industry with inventories and style-changes and seasons and strikes and programming and hardware and software and imports and prices and shipping time and even nepotism, for that matter. (As it stands now these are words on reports and little more.) Then, upon completion of an apprenticeship in the real world and their hiring by a member of the New York Stock Exchange, the trainee would work a minimum of six months in the main branch's back office on Wall Street. He would handle certificates in the securities cage; process dividends; hunt for lost stocks; find out about our industry's problems and where possibly to get to the heart of them. *Then and only then* should come the current six-month training schedule of rules and regulations and what-is-a-stock and what-is-a-bond and the other pap that no trainee ever remembers past the exam to get him registered. Only if methods like this are adopted will the industry even come close to being a profession. The brokers who make it through this regimen will make a great deal of money. But it will wash out most of the fakers and hustlers, the sons and sons-in-law, the lazy and the misfits. The survivors will make a great deal of money but they'll have earned it. People bitch about their brokers now. And they complain about their doctors and *their* money; their lawyers and *their* money. At least stockbrokers should get an education approximating medical school or law school. Perhaps someday *we* can have Keogh Plans also. And play golf on Wednesdays.

How good is brokerage house research? In most cases it's not worth the time spent on it, nor the time spent reading it. Here's how many research reports evolve. The research partner smokes his pipe and says to his staff, "Gentlemen and lady (usually there is one lady analyst per staff and usually she is the transportation specialist; God knows why, unless it is to explode the myth of the typical woman driver), how about a rundown on the paper industry?"

Two analysts go on a field trip to visit Kimberly-Clark, Scott Paper, International Paper and St. Regis. They talk with management, take notes (trying to read between the lines, since management is not allowed to be specific about anything, according to the SEC) and watch the paper industry in progress.

"See our modernization programs taking hold," they are told by the vice-presidents who escort them. "See our new up-to-the-minute equipment, our computers working around the clock. One thing computers don't do is sleep."

"Impressive," say the analysts. "Very impressive."

"And our efforts in the conservation-ecology fields. Every time we cut a tree down, we plant two more."

"Impressive. You've certainly taken great strides," the analysts say, taking notes.

"Now then, you fellows staying overnight here in Neenah, Wisconsin? No? Well don't hesitate to ask if we folk here can make your stay more comfortable."

The analysts hit four companies in three days including the Sandusky, Ohio, plant turning out Cut Rite wax paper. They pad the gasoline and mileage and dinner bills, come back to New York and write a six-page report titled "The Turnaround Possibilities in the Paper Industry." The re-

port is condensed to three pages, announced to all the salesmen in the firm in advance of nationwide advertising, so
that the salesmen can tell their clients in effect: "We're doing a report on International Paper. How about taking
advantage before we release it and the price maybe goes
up. Our reports carry a lot of weight on the Street."

The customer buys, convinced that he is on to some-
thing that smacks of "the inside." The report breaks and
International Paper is up a quarter of a point that day. St.
Regis is off an eighth, and we hear the old Wall Street story
"Scott Paper touches new bottoms."

So-called "institutional reports," which presume to be
strictly "for the professional investor," are the same six-
page effort, fleshed out to twelve pages and bound in a
colorful binder for the status-conscious institutions who in
boom times believe they can tell a book by its cover and in
bust periods are incapable of telling anything.

The *best* research can be done by the individual investor
who buys products by habit in retail stores, gas stations,
restaurants, pharmacies. Notice the labels on the national
brands you buy. Ask your bank whose computers they
use and whether they work efficiently. Ask your doctor
which drug companies he prefers. (That's the *only* question
relating to the stock market you should ever ask your
doctor; and always get supporting opinion from at least
one other of his colleagues.) Ask your dentist whose equipment *he* uses, and if you're building a home, ask your
builder whose products he buys and why. You can be your
own best stock analyst.

This approach is at least as effective as a field trip report
from researchers who gather together at luncheons to fete

visiting executives and hurl thunderbolts of jargon at the public that deserve C minus for style, straight C for content. There are no *guts* in research reports from most brokerage houses and you cannot beat a gut reaction in an analysis of a company. If *you* like a product and buy it, and your friends buy it, check the manufacturer. More than likely it is a company that is publicly traded, and millions of other people use the product. Try this system once. You'll never read another brokerage report, and there will be an awful lot of security analysts who will be forced from pipes to rolling their own. If there are any doubters, I have a maiden aunt who bought Tampax at 12, Revlon at 20 and Mary Kay at 17 (before it went to 62). She never married, incidentally.

Michael, the ex media rep, came back from lunch and said that he saw an old client of ours through the window of a serve-yourself cafeteria. The client was a nuisance, one of the lost souls who haunt boardrooms of brokerage houses, taking up space and never entering orders except once or twice a year. (And then he'd buy 200 shares of a $3 stock just to maintain his seat at the front of the room.) This character we called "the Slinker." He'd push the door to our office in and creep an arm around the corner, then his head, then a leg. Very slowly. Then he'd run to the Dow-Jones news machine and preempt the space in front of it, flipping through the rolls of paper, taking notes in a notebook the size of a pocket dictionary which he never let anyone look into. At the end of the day, he'd check wastebaskets for discarded *Wall Street Journals,* adjourn to the men's room across the hall, where he would do everything but take a bath, pin his thinning hair together in strands with hairpins—yes, that's right, hairpins—and slink off to some cafeteria to study the *Journal* and check on his notebook scribbling. Right out of Sherwood Anderson. The Slinker had another disconcerting habit. After he lunged for the Dow-Jones ticker, he would greet anyone in his way. "Good aftermorning," he would say. "Have a strong day."

But hairpins in the washbasins of the men's room was the final straw. I advised the Slinker, back in mid-1968, that we were too busy to have him taking up our chairs and that he had no salvage rights to our *Wall Street Journals*. He slunk away.

Michael, the ex media rep, was triumphant after seeing the Slinker through the restaurant window. "He was eating a sandwich he had carried in with him," I was told. "Wrapped in wax paper and an elastic band." (The Slinker ordered milk or tea in cafeterias, but always brought his own food.) "I made a little sign," Michael went on, "and rapped on the window. The Slinker looked up and smiled because the sign said COME BACK. WE NEED THE BUSINESS. Time was always on the side of the Slinker," said Michael. "And we never knew it."

The market closed today down 13.48 at 675.66 and the Dow-Jones ticker says: THERE IS NO FURTHER SUPPORT ABOVE THE OLD LOWS.

5.

In the Laps of the Gods

Wednesday, July 8:

To aid us in our hours of trial, we receive over the Tele-type each morning an Advisory Service Letter, consisting of a paragraph of sermon and a capsule recommendation of three or four Stocks for Action. Our pundit's sermons have been getting longer and his stock list shorter ever since he mentioned Penn Central at 40, Twentieth Century Fox at 42 and U.S. Steel at 38, among others, as Buys. Today he must be considering encounter-group assistance, beginning his cheery greeting with "Down and down they go," and ending with "Gloom and despair have taken over."

I read the sports and the comics in both local newspapers, avoiding the headlines, and turned to the classified section of the *Wall Street Journal*. Anything to put off the inevitable. There was a large advertisement for a franchise I hadn't seen yet: Mickey Rooney's Fun 'n' Game Room, which ranks right up there along with Roger Williams's Music Centers, Jerry Lewis's Cinemas and Hoss Cartwright's Bonanza Steak Houses. I found myself wondering why there wasn't a Tommy Manville Bride Shop franchise or Lucky Luciano's Pizza and Knuckle Sandwich Shoppes. Nothing surprises me when it comes to the tail end of a trend.

Let me tell you about concept stocks and "fads" in the marketplace. When a fad's number is up, absurdity sets in. This is why we're now seeing Mickey Rooney trying to cash in, or rather *someone* trying to cash in on the Rooney name. (Mickey probably has his own Fun 'n' Game Room). At the rate we were going a year ago, there would have been a Fried Chicken Take-out place on every corner in America. And dozens of companies went public, doubled and tripled in price, by the mere virtue of being in a popular area. You *can* make money by following trends, and certainly some of the companies in the field (McDonald's Hamburgers and Friendly Ice Cream, for example) are well managed and well conceived and will, I feel sure, survive. Most of the others are too late with much too little, with the initiators skimming off whatever cream there was and leaving the poor stockbrokers and the poorer franchisees to lick their wounds and their remaining beefburgers in silence. When the classified section of every newspaper offered page upon page of franchise opportunities, you knew the end was in sight.

I learned my lesson long ago when the two bowling stocks Brunswick and American Machine & Foundry (AMF) were chasing each other up the price-and-profit ladder and were the darlings of Wall Street. Brunswick was the first stock I bought for myself when I came into the brokerage business. I bought three shares at 74¼ (74⅞ was the all-time high price). "What can stop it going to 100 again?" I reasoned. "Isn't everyone a bowler? Millions of people? And a bowling alley will be on every corner in the United States. Not to mention the possibilities abroad." Of course, I personally hadn't been in a bowling alley since I was sixteen and only then to romance the girl who rented the bowling shoes. She wore the tightest sweaters with the best reasons for wearing the tightest sweaters in my hometown.

I sold my Brunswick at 58 and it went to 6, and AMF went from 63 to 17. Dozens of imitators went out of business entirely, and another fad went the way of the Hula Hoop and the Twist. The same fate, in varying degrees, befell electronics stocks in the early 1960's, and later insurance companies, color television manufacturers (remember National Video?), airlines, conglomerates, nursing homes, and dozens of other groups bulled along by greed and romantic visions. Most investors and speculators miss the beginning of these trends, but that's all right. The single, most important concept to learn in regard to the stock market is when to sell. Buying is easy; it's selling that takes a knack, and detachment is the key to selling. Remember this: stocks, especially stocks in the midst of a fad, always go higher than you would think, because the enthusiasm of the believers always works in patterns of hysteria that move stocks beyond the realm of reality. The reverse is also always true. When out of favor, stocks go lower than anyone believes they will.

"How low is low?" is a question customers have asked me over the years when something they bought at 20 sells at 5. The answer is, if the reasons you bought the stock at 20 still exist, probably you should buy more at 5. The typical *over*reaction has forced it lower than anyone expected. But my rule on buying and selling these fad stocks is to buy the leaders in the field, the biggest companies with the most exposure. Institutions are most likely to be in *these* companies, because generally those companies have the greatest amount of stock outstanding and the funds can take large positions. Funds love to take large positions and chase each other up the tape.

Always follow the big boys *part* of the way up. When you can count fifteen or more companies in the field moving up to high ground, and *most* important, when you are getting tips on $7 to $12 stocks in the same field *over-the-counter,* that's the time to unload. You might be early, and the trend for nursing homes or youth marketing or conglomerates may spiral upwards for another few months or even half a year. But when they start down, it's Maggie, bar the door. Nothing is more difficult than to get out with your skin when the funds are raping the public with their dumping and are switching their teen-age portfolio managers like linen in a whorehouse. Don't fall in love with a concept; none of them last, not even Ecology. And never agonize over selling a stock. I guarantee that in every kind of stock-market climate, whether bullish or in the depths of the Bear's den, when you sell something, your broker will be able to recommend a new stock to purchase.

Believe it. You can call your stockbroker in any situation and ask him, "How's business?"

And he will say, "Horrible. Nixon is stifling the country; there's a bomb in every office building; pollution is rampant; and there's such discontent that I've taken an option on ten acres near the Costa Brava."

"Well, do you *like* anything? I've got about $5,000 I'd like to invest."

"Sure," the broker says. "I've got an interesting situation, around $12, near the low. I've just seen some awfully big money move into it."

Don't worry if you've just sold a stock. We've always got something for you to buy.

Since the horses you can ride as an investor are without number, let me say a few more things about the physical act of buying and selling stocks. *First of all, set an objective for yourself and make it a realistic objective.* When you're told by someone to buy ABC at 10, because it's going to 30, that's all right. Ridiculous, but all right. Buy it if you like, but if it hits 15, run like a thief. That's 50 per cent on your money, right? On a tip, right? Don't be a pig. But it's all right to be a pig as long as you're not a damn fool. You'll find out early in your investment/speculative experience that no stock bought on a tip ever reaches the objectives set for it by the tipper. Then why such outrageous stories about buying a stock at 10 because it's going to 30? Because tips need embellishment in order to be promoted successfully. It's like telling a friend to go out with a certain girl, a dog, because she's a sure thing on the first date. She *may* be a sure thing on the *fifth* date. If you hang around that long. And the stock *may* go to 30 if you live long enough. But speculators *or* investors buying on a tip are not noted for their patience.

When I buy a stock for investment on my analysis (not a tip), I set a point objective that I think reasonable based on two things: (a) its price history in relation to its earnings, and (b) my feeling about the likelihood that the public will jump on the bandwagon of that particular stock once it starts to move. I bought 200 Cenco Instruments for myself today at 19 and have a mental objective for it of 29⅞ a share sometime in the next year. That's almost 11 points, approximately 50 per cent on my money. If the market improves, some of the older glamour stocks will improve by mere attrition. I pick Cenco because it's well managed and traditionally is firm in strong markets. Twenty-nine and seven-eighths is probably too *low* an objective. But I'll be glad to pass it on to someone at that price who thinks it's cheap. Over 30 for the stock is a price area in the laps of the gods, where I can no longer assess the stock according to my formulas for value. Natomas over 100 was in this category; also Inflight Motion Pictures at 40, Litton or Ling-Temco over 100, University Computing ditto, and hundreds of others *you* yourself could name which sell, at times in their careers' way, *way* over the point that anyone not institutionalized or working for hedge funds could buy with any degree of certainty. One of my best clients sold out to a company then selling at 63 and earning fifty cents a share. He urged me to buy some of the stock because management had told him it would be at 1,000 in three years.

"A thousand?" I said, horrified. "Guarantee me *seventy* a share and you've got a deal."

"We've got plans," he said. "No one can stop us."

In 1969, my client's division was the only one in the black. Now the parent company has taken his cash. The stock presently shows a deficit of over $1 a share and sells for 4.

"Do you think management will make their target of 1,000 on time?" I asked him last week. "They've got about a year to do it, and I'd like to tell my customers."

"I *do* think we can be selling at 10 in the next year," he told me. "With any luck and a few government contracts."

"Well. That's more than a double," I said hopefully. "In business your reach should always exceed your grasp."

He nodded as if he had never heard *that* one before, and wishing he still owned his own company. He is no longer one of my best clients.

And this is a brilliant businessman, *in his own field*, who knows what it takes to make a buck. And he *believed* that the stock would go to 1,000. That is the most unbelievable thing of all: the fact that wealthy people, who may even go to church, raise their children to respect God and country, cheat on the wives only when out of town, can pay prices for stocks that discount earnings ten and fifteen *years* into the wild, blue future.

Do you remember the song "It's Only a Paper Moon"? If you believe in that song you have a shot at making money in the stock market. When you can*not* find *three reasons* for holding a stock (I won't count the chartists' jargon "because it's going up" as a valid reason), then the price of the stock is "in the laps of the gods," and eventually supply and demand will find you praying to those gods for mercy. And to break you even.

In picking objectives for selling Cenco, why did I say 29⅞? Why not 30, an even figure? Because very often a stock will touch 29⅞ or 39⅞ or 99⅞ and that will be the high point. If it hits 30 or 40 or 100, it usually triggers new buying and new interest, and goes higher. I always give away $12.50 (an eighth of a point per 100 shares) to insure selling my merchandise when I believe it has gone high enough. And I *always* sell when there is enthusiasm for a stock, when it's active and moving up.

I have one particular client who goes into shock when making a decision to sell. He enters when I call CIC orders. Cancel If Close. He'll put in an order to sell 500 XYZ at 25, having paid 21 for the stock. When it hits 24¾, he'll cancel the order. This is typical of this client and many others who feel that if it's acting so well they're going to hold out for 27. Then the volume dries up and the stock slips to 24. "Put it in at 25 again," they say. The stock goes to 23¼.

"Lower it to 24," they say.

Selling hits the stock and it drops back to 22½.

"Sell the goddamn thing," they say, suddenly intrigued by something else. They wind up with 22 for 100 shares, 21¾ for the rest, but they never learn their lesson. It is easy to sell your stock when a lot of people are eager for it. If your profit is there and the stock is strong, *give* it to someone who wants it so badly. On balance, when trading, *you* will be the person who's right. Never mind the story about your cousin who owned Polaroid at 3, who if he had held on to it would be worth $500,000 today. Everyone has stories like this and they're meaningless. The Big Hit is one in a million, and I'm writing this book to let you know how to make money, year in and year out, by treating your stocks as numbers, not as your children. The cousin who owned Polaroid at 3 saw it go to 6 and doubled his money. Terrific. Then to 9 for a triple; sold it at 9½, tickled to death, but anxious to buy an issue in the relatively new (then) field of converting atomic energy to civilian use. Not one person in ten thousand would have had the foresight, or the stomach, to hold Polaroid all these years. Don't agonize over these stories. I'm trying to get you 20 per cent on your money (sometimes more, sometimes a little less) *every* year. And I'm talking about capital gains, not including dividends.

Can the Big Hit be made? There *are* ways, which I shall discuss later on. Mostly they are too dull for the average investor, who must have short-term action. So be prepared. Big Hits are only made over the long term, and the closer you watch a favorite of yours the worse you will do. I took a loser off someone's hands three years ago, doing him a favor for his tax purposes. I bought from him 3,000 shares of Major Realty (a Florida land developer) over-the-counter, for eleven cents a share. In three months it was sixty-five cents, and I sold it so fast it would have made your head swim. I spent the proceeds on a seven-course dinner in an obscenely private dining room, tipping everyone from the sommelier to the pastry chef. Ahhh, those were the days, when the Dow was poised to break through

1,000; God was in his heaven and you could ride a turkey (if not a Fried Chicken) to retirement. Major Realty a year later was selling at *twelve dollars* a share. But I would have had to be hospitalized in a coma to have held it that long. So would your cousin with Polaroid. *He who looks back at the market dies of remorse!*

In giving lessons on selling stock, I must tell you about pools on over-the-counter companies. How they work, and how you can be aware of them (despite the regulatory agencies — SEC, NASD, New York Stock Exchange rules, and so forth), and possibly make money (despite yourself). Two stories come to mind of pertinent issues that I have traded in the last few years. Situations like these have existed in every major city. You can fill in the promotions of your choice.

The first story was brought north from Florida and it employed standard embellishment: a glamorous product (revolutionary diet drink) and big names surrounding it. (Usually you are told that there's Rockefeller money in there, or Murchison from Texas, or that ITT is looking at them.) Well, everyone coming up from Florida in this particular year had this stock, buying it at 3 and 4, telling tales of it going to 20. The company issued PR releases at 5, and brokers in Florida called existing stockholders, urging them to double up. Many people did, and the same buyers urged *their* friends and relatives to buy. (No one likes to be in a promotion alone. If they *make* money, they'll have the satisfaction of being in the stock earlier than their friends. If they *lose* money, it will be almost more satisfactory because they won't have to go down the

drain without familiar company. I begged one of my customers who bought it at 4 to sell at 8, and he told me, "I'll
either sell at 20 or at nothing." Two years later he used it
for a tax loss, needing a letter from me "To whom it may
concern" (I presume it concerned the Internal Revenue
Service) letting him know that there was no market and no
stated value for the stock. (A year after that his own shoe
factories closed their doors, but that's another story.) The
soft-drink concern, despite the public relations blurbs and
the promotions, folded fast. But it was discovered later
that *insiders* had been selling *their* stock at 4 and 5, just
when they had been singing its praises to the public. At
least one officer of the company went to jail. He owned
the stock at ten cents.

The only time promotions of this sort can work is when
there is volume or activity in the stock. Promoters cannot
sell in a dead market; they need frenzy. Forget the Securities and Exchange Commission, the bureaucrat-ridden
toothless tiger. There are all kinds of ways to bypass the
law, with relatives and friends and stock issued in straw
names. *You cannot legislate human nature. Greed will
find a way.* If you do ever buy a stock like the soft-drink
company, or companies with cures for bad breath, baldness, or the blues, and you pay $2 having been told that it's
going to 10, get out at 4 to 6. You can sure you're getting
out with the friends of the management. While they're
working in the prison printshop learning a trade, *you* can
be out looking for new stock promotions.

The second story involves one city, where the situation
springs from wealthy people in that city with a reputation
for magic and money. "He falls into manure and comes

up smelling like a rose." You know the kind. Everyone hates them and wishes them ill. But everyone is ready to jump in the manure after them, hoping some rosewater will rub off. A money man of this sort took over the corporate shell (a few million shares he bought at five cents a share) of a company that had been public, merged it with his own company, and it became traded immediately over-the-counter. Suddenly I was deluged with buy orders at seventy-five cents, then $1, then $1.50, and promoters of the company, friends of management and hustling stockbrokers, bulled the stock to 3, then 4, on rumors of profits, further acquisitions and the reputation of the largest stockholder, who fell into sewers and came up smelling as you might expect. The stock went to 8, then collapsed. But a lot of people made money on what was in essence nothing but mass hysteria. The tipoff comes, in this case, from the small buyer. A rule: *if you hear a rumor, especially on an over-the-counter stock that many people you know claim to own, and you have enough money to buy 50 or 75 shares, Don't!* That's the top. The promotion is over. When I get orders to buy 50 shares of a stock that is 7 and was 3 a month ago, it's the beginning of the end. *If* you buy 50 or 75 shares of *anything* on a tip, you can be sure you've been the last to know.

If you do buy a stock too high, where is the best place to buy more or average your cost? Or should you average your cost? Most institutions do *not* average their purchases. If stocks go down, they either sit it out or dump. Why is this? I asked a portfolio manager, a sometime customer of mine, who helps invest for a $60 million fund.

"Because of American Motors, we never average stocks down," he said.

"American Motors?"

"We loved it at 14½ and bought a slug of it. The Gremlin was going to revolutionize the nation's automobile-buying habits. Then we loved it at 10. We *had* to buy more at 8 because we were hooked so badly. We've tried to hawk our position to every pension fund and university in the country and there are no takers. Now we hear American Motors may not survive 1971 and there may be gremlins in the chassis of the Gremlin. The investment committee will allow no more averaging down, and the analysts who pushed us into it have been given the assignment of clipping items from the trade journals about companies we watch. With scissors. And filing them in our files."

"Siberia," I said.

"You can be wrong in this business," he told me. "But you better not be wrong *big*."

Individual investors rarely average stocks, either because they don't have any more available funds, or because they're terrified of sending good money after bad. Yet as a rule, you can *always* average quality companies on the way down and eventually make money. Or at least recover your cost.

Let me illustrate: if you buy a stock at 20 and it's now selling at 10, take a long, dispassionate look at the company. If reasoning *without emotion* tells you that the stock appears to have overreacted on the downside, do not be afraid to buy more. It's a long road back to 20, with people probably selling all along the way. But 15 is a much closer and realistic objective. Stocks seldom recover all of their lost ground, but they very often get halfway back. With money I handle on a discretionary basis, I always leave some surplus funds to average out stocks that go lower. This is a most important idea for those of you with *limited* resources. If you have $5,000 to invest and you want to buy *XYZ* at 25, buy 100 shares now and hold the rest of the money back in reserve. If the stock backs off to the 20–22 area, consider buying more. If the stock *never* backs off, and continues higher, at least you own 100 shares. If you commit only part of your cash at one price, you allow yourself more flexibility. And flexibility is the key to success for the average investor with $2,000 to $50,000. Find yourself a stockbroker who can work with you on this formula, for flexibility is the key to a successful investment adviser as well. Your money has no business being in the hands of anyone else.

Our morning forecaster observed that "gloom and doom have taken over." As a result, the market rallied sharply today, closing up 12.60 on increasing volume.

I had two customers in during the day who are symptomatic of the times. One client, in the construction business, is always in coveralls and hard hat. He owns his own business, which grosses $2.5 million a year, but loves the workingman image.

"A seat on the Big Board," I told him, "sold today for $140,000. Off from $540,000 just two years ago."

"I don't wonder," he said. "Who the hell wants to put money into a losing business? What do you think, there's a Santa Claus? An easy way to get rich? Let me tell you what's happening in this country. There's a guy I did a big job for, $100,000 for roads in a development. Tells me he won't pay his bill. 'Sue me,' he says. 'With interest rates what they are — and it won't come to trial for a year — I'll make money on the deal.' Can you imagine the son-of-a-bitch? I'd break both his arms if I thought it would do any good. This is what's happening today. The little guy is getting squeezed to the wall. And nobody gives a damn."

My second customer is a rock musician, a player of chords on a $400 electric guitar, and he's mostly unemployed. Luckily, he came into a sizable inheritance, enough to afford him a psychiatrist to find excuses for his not being employed *and* to get him out of the draft. But every month he brings in a certificate for 100 Gillette, or 100 Ford Motor or 100 Warner-Lambert, sells 10 or 15 shares and has the rest returned to him, along with our check for the proceeds. Today he is blowing grass. No one knows except me, but the customer smells like the checking station at the Nuevo Laredo border. He has a girl with him, long-haired and lovely in an innocent way. She is nodding her head in time to the clattering of the ticker tapes. A new beat.

"What can you get me now for 10 Gillette, man?" he said.

"Around 45," I told him, "if we sold right away."

"Try and get 45½," he said, being a true odd-lotter.

"How soon do you need the money?"

"Yesterday, man," he said.

"Then don't fool around for half a point. You want to sell it, sell it."

"Go ahead, man. Just don't get me the low of the day."
He tapped his cigarette into my ashtray.

"Any gigs on the horizon?" I asked him. (They tell me gig is musician language for a job.)

"A few possibles. Goin' to see some cats now, looking for a lead guitar."

I put in the 10 Gillette to sell at the market. And the rich kid left with his girl. When the Gillette runs out, he'll be in Daddy's business faster than you can say marijuana. Middle-class is flashing all over him like the hairs on his chinny-chin-chin.

Perhaps there's hope for the market.

Thursday, July 9, through Friday, July 17:

Everyone gets excited in good markets, and sentiment changes with the hum of increasing volume. You will find that in good markets, Bull markets, any bad news is shrugged off, discounted, and set aside, while stocks continue higher. In Bear markets there is no positive reaction to good news other than an occasional half-hearted rally. Judge news that you read in the papers and see on television *only* in light of the market in general. Don't be afraid to do some independent thinking.

Wild Bob the Bear called on Thursday with buy orders in Natomas at 50 and Control Data at 32. "It's not how many scores you make on the top," he rasped at me, "it's how you come screaming off the bottom. Joe Kennedy shorted all the way down in 1930. His partners thought he was flaky. Getty borrowed $25,000 at the bottom. He was broke. This is a rally in a Bear market, so don't get excited," he said, still rasping. "A temporary bounce." Bob and his group were now trying to peddle their services to mutual funds and insurance companies, selling their commentary for fees ranging from $1,000 to $5,000 *per stock* that they analyzed. "Put the orders in," he yelled at me, and hung up. The market was getting stronger.

"The economy has hit bottom," says the resident partner, "but it will not show up for three or four months. The Federal Reserve is making money more available. It's reflected in the weekly figures in the *Times*. And I think interest rates have peaked. Buy the money-sensitive stocks; I'm going out for coffee."

Basically, who makes the market stronger when conditions have been so stagnant? It is a mass movement, the technique of herds in panic. Institutions initiate a rally. Mutual funds, pension plans, insurance companies start to nibble at what they believe to be bargains. Markets are so thin that stock prices begin to move up quickly. This brings other institutions in from the sidelines who cannot afford to have their funds idle in the event that the rally is real. In three days (Wednesday the eighth, Thursday the ninth, Friday the tenth) the Dow Jones average is up 30 points, closing the week of July 6 over the 700 level. Institutions can initiate a rally, but the public *must* come in to sustain it.

Over the weekend I played in a golf tournament. There are 11 million golfers in the United States today and they will spend $2.8 billion on the sport this year. There is no better place to take a sampling of public sentiment on the stock market than in a golf-course locker room. I get some of my best information there. The consensus among businessmen I talked with was that there was hope of the economy turning for the better as we looked forward to spring 1971. A lot of people were suddenly interested in the stock market, people who hadn't moved their money in nine or ten months.

I took orders for 4,000 shares of various companies while having a beer in the locker room on Sunday. This included 1,000 shares from a new account, the president of a public company.

"How's his handicap?" I asked one of the locker-room attendants.

"Plays from an eighteen," I was told. "But he drinks to scratch. He's never farther than a wedge from a bottle of vodka. Confidentially, if he shakes hand with you, count your fingers when he leaves."

I wasn't very worried about getting paid for the stock. People can be four-flushers, adulterers and thieves in their business dealings. But they are gentlemen at their clubs. No one who plays in a regular foursome can bear to be socially unacceptable. I bought the stock for him on Monday. Wednesday I received a check. I called to thank him. "People do not pay this promptly," I said. "It's a pleasure to do business with you."

"It cost me three days' interest, but I wanted to get off on the right foot. After all, we're both in the club."

I had the check and my fingers were all there.

Customers often complain about the payment rules of brokerage houses and the New York Stock Exchange. People must pay for securities by the fifth business day after a trade. (This is called the "value date.") They are also supposed to deliver securities that have been sold by the fifth business day in order to get paid on time.

I've often heard this complaint: "We get telegrams if you don't get *your* money right away. But we can go whistle for *ours*. We never get paid on time. Why does the customer always get screwed?"

You must understand that we are a highly regulated business, with red tape, stupidity and new rules becoming more of a problem every month. Each major brokerage firm has a compliance department, whose sole function is to supervise and supplement the regulations of the SEC, the New York Stock Exchange, the National Association of Securities Dealers and its own individual company house rules. We need files for our files to keep all the memos straight.

Why this tremendous growth in regulatory policies? The reasons are twofold: first, to protect the public; second, to prevent our complete takeover by the federal government or our subjection to the kinds of rules by which a public utility must operate.

If you want your money on the fifth day, send in your securities in good delivery form. This means signing them on the back, on the space provided, exactly where you ordinarily would sign a letter. You can send your stock *regular* mail if you take this precaution: there is a line on the back of every certificate that says "and do hereby irrevocably constitute and appoint _____ attorney"; fill in the name of the brokerage firm that sold your stock in the space *before* "attorney." This makes the certificate nonnegotiable and you save yourself the nuisance of registered mail. Don't be sloppy with your money.

If your stock is in joint name (husband and wife or whatever), tell your broker whose name the stock is in *before you sell it*. Then *both* of you sign the reverse side. If the stock is in the name of a corporation, each time you sell a stock the individual transfer agent (the bank that disburses dividends and distributes certificates) wants to see a copy of the corporate resolution allowing you to act for the company. It is not the broker who needs these papers, it is the bank. Don't foam at the mouth about your money not being paid you on time. Learn the rules that restrict your broker. We do not operate in the atmosphere of a manufacturing or retail business. But if you've done everything according to form and you are *still* unsatisfied, don't waste time with your broker. Go where there is some clout: the manager, officer, or resident partner. They can get you some action because someone in the back office will listen to them. Most registered representatives are terrible about following up problems. They just want to write orders. We had gotten very spoiled until 1969.

The week of July 13:

Institutions are becoming terrified that they are missing out on something and the phones are ringing again. Funds wanted to dump *any* of last year's mistakes and buy anything that was moving or might move. Mostly blue chips, quality companies out of favor for some time. But the volume was still low.

According to Sonny Huber, the former butcher, "There's no public business. I can't raise 10 shares and I've been on the phone for two days. All I can say is that I wasn't born here, but I'm sure dyin' here." The market was up over 30 points this week to close at 735.08, a recovery high from the bottom of 631 in May.

Manny, the Hard Rider, called me from Butte, Montana, at four-thirty and I knew the public could not be far away. Manny, a good customer of mine, had been responsible for a family trust of $1.5 million and a family company profit-sharing plan of half a million. He loaded both portfolios with thousands of shares of over-the-counter dogs, none of which could now be sold without wiping out the trusts. So Manny took a leave of absence, presumably for six months. "The pressure and all the family crap," he had said. "I need to clear the cobwebs. I'm single, no responsibilities other than to the business. There's a lot of country to see and life is too short." So Manny took off in his leased Lincoln Continental with vanity plates spelling MANNY to find America.

"I scored last night," he told me. "A waitress in the best restaurant in Butte, if you can believe it. She had never been for a ride in a Continental before."

"Are you finding America?" I asked him.

"I've been gone a month and I already miss the business," he said. "But I'm going to score in every state before I come back. That's what America means to me. By the way, got a tip. Look up General Aircraft. Sells around a buck. I've been thinking of some switches. . . ."

6.

A Spoonful of Sugar
and Bernie Baruch

Monday, July 20:

Some of the oppressive gloom of the past five months
has lifted. The morning commentary in the *Journal* from
other brokerage houses and the advisory services is uni-
formly good. President Nixon says that the business cycle
has bottomed out and he sees full employment by next
July first.

"The vast majority of stocks have seen their lows," says
Shearson Hammill, the brokerage firm, and Shearson Hammill is echoed by the $20 million Knickerbocker Fund,
who say, "we are experiencing a reversal of the *nineteen-
month-long* Bear market."

I told all this to a woman customer who called to check on a dividend she was missing.

"There's only two things I want," she said to me.

"Your dividend and a stock that doubles," I said.

"Wrong," she told me. "I want looks and luck. That's all. The key to understanding what every woman wants. Looks and luck."

Bearing that in mind, I read this morning that for the first time since 1952, men have overtaken women as stockholders: 15.7 million men to 15.2 million women. There is so much to say about women investors and women in the stock market that I will devote further sections to the subject as we go on. But I must give you an example of the kind of metabolic changes women undergo in relation to their money, Germaine Greer to the contrary notwithstanding.

I gave a lecture a few years ago and received a phone call the following week from a woman who had attended. Selma Cuffe was her name.

"I think you can be of assistance to me," she said. "I've never made a nickel in the market. I've never received anything but runarounds. You don't give runarounds, do you?"

She had approximately $6,000 to invest and came to me with a tax-loss carry-forward of about $4,000 which she was desperate to make up. I concentrated on lower-priced (under 15) issues, local companies where I was familiar with management and which I felt were cheap. We made up almost $2,500 in a short time, and I doubled up on a company in the leased department-discount store field — let's call it Super Rack — buying 1,000 shares for

Mrs. Cuffe at 5. It sat at 5 for four months and Mrs. Cuffe called me every day. "So what's the story?" she'd ask. "Don't tell me it's 5 again."

"A stock is not like a roast, Mrs. Cuffe," I told her. "It's not *done* in so many minutes."

"Look, I don't want to be buried in that thing, Super-whatever-it-is. First time it moves and I clear a little, get me out."

Shortly thereafter, in a two-day span, Super Rack jumped 1¼ points. I sold her out, netting around a $950 profit. And I bought another company in the same field that had had the same trading pattern for years: dull for long periods, followed by a sudden spurt, like the Seven-Year Itch. There are dozens of stocks like this, mostly on the American Exchange, that are always buys when they drift to 5 or 6 on no volume. Usually, within a few months sudden buying pushes them ahead 2 or 3 points and you can get out. These are bread-and-butter stocks. A dull way to make 40 per cent on your money, but it's relatively safe and a great method for cutting down the odds.

When I bought the next stock for Mrs. Cuffe (she had given me full discretionary power) I went over the proceeds from the last sale by about $120. This was no problem. On her instructions I was always to round out a purchase to the next round lot (1,000 shares instead of 985, et cetera). The next day Super Rack, the stock we had sold, moved up a point and a half. I couldn't believe the sudden strength, but Mrs. Cuffe could. She called. "Oh my God," she said. "That Super-stock. Up another 2 points. You didn't sell it, did you?"

"I told you I sold it, Mrs. Cuffe. We bought Jobbers International in the same field."

"Oh my God. You lost me $1,500."

"I *made* you $950. You wanted to get out of Super Rack. You were bored with it, remember?"

"But I never thought it would move so fast, Brutus. You should have known."

I'm always patient with hysterical women. But I don't know why. Yes I do. If you're *not* patient, they go to the SEC. The thought-police are everywhere in this business.

Mrs. Cuffe calmed down eventually and I told her I was leaving for London the next day to visit the queen and frighten a little mouse under the chair. "*You* handle her account?" she asked.

"In a manner of speaking," I said.

"Well. It's my New Year," she said. "Rosh Hashanah, the Jewish New Year. I'll be in temple a lot this week. I'll wish *you* a Happy New Year and one to what-do-you-call it, Jobbers International."

I felt I had done my duty, but in *her* early hysteria, and my response, I forgot to tell her to send in the $120 overage on the purchase. London was so civilized and such fun, I neglected to go into my office on Threadneedle Street until the end of the week, and only then to close out some Amphenol I had bought for myself before leaving the States.

"Messages for you, sir," a clerk said to me.

"Your name Cratchit?" I asked.

"What, sir?" he said. "Oh, I get it. Cratchit. Very good sir."

I didn't want to be abroad and not let everyone know that there were still ugly Americans.

There were six or seven Telex messages for me, from the home office, mostly reports of the business I had done, and one with exclamation points from my secretary. SENT SELL-OUT TELEGRAM, it read, TO MRS. CUFFE FOR $120. SHE RECEIVED IT ON YOM KIPPUR AND HAS CALLED HER ATTORNEYS. CAN YOU STAND IT?"

I crumpled the wire and walked out of my London office to have a pint of bitters and some sausage. When in Rome.

When I got back to the States I faced up to the situation and called Mrs. Cuffe. Jobbers International was a quarter point below where we had bought it; Super Rack was still up over a point from where we had sold.

"You've pierced me to my heart," she said. "On our holiest day. In temple, God help me. When I'm supposed to be atoning for my sins of the last year, all I could think of was the Super-something up another point and me losing out on $1,500. God forgive me. And then that telegram. Who died? I thought. Scaring me out of my wits on the holiest day of the year for one hundred and twenty stinking dollars. We're not even supposed to *read* on that day."

I apologized for not telling her earlier.

"I've decided my lawyer can do nothing, so I've canceled him. But God forgive you for making me think of that Super-stock on our holiest day."

I swore never to take another woman client.

The next day I received in the mail a note from Mrs. Cuffe.

I'm sure that you must have many Jewish clients. I'm enclosing a copy of this year's Hebrew calendar. For you to refer to and not bother us on the wrong days. There is always room to learn. Good luck in the future.

Your ex-pupil,

Selma

Mrs. Harold Cuffe

All the holy days were marked in red circles. Also enclosed, along with the calendar, were instructions to transfer her account to Merrill Lynch. So it goes.

I went to tell the story to the resident partner, because there is one recurring theme in the brokerage business for the last five years: keep nothing to yourself. Tell everyone everything or you're liable to find your name in the New York Stock Exchange bulletin as a horrible example.

The kindly old gentleman sat me down. "There's no accounting for how people will act," he said. "Did I ever tell you the one about Bernie Baruch?"

"Tell me again."

"Baruch gave a young stockbroker a chance to handle some money for him. The first few trades the young broker executed lost money. He came to Baruch and begged his forgiveness, offering apologies and excuses.

" 'Remember one thing, young man,' Baruch had said, 'if you're going to survive in this business. *You cannot be God for a commission!*' "

"That's a good story," I told the partner. "But I'm sorry about Mrs. Cuffe. It's like a surgeon losing a patient."

III

"She just went to Merrill Lynch," he said. "She's not dead."

I raised my eyebrows and made the sign of the cross.

Thursday, July 23:

Gardner Ackley, former economic adviser to President Johnson, says, "we cannot rule out the possibility of a severe *depression*." But despite Democratic gloom-sayers, it has been a good trading market for a few weeks with the chance to move in and out, with some degree of flexibility for a change.

At eleven-thirty the trust department of the city's largest bank has just called me with some directed orders. "Buy 50 IBM, 100 Xerox, 100 Polaroid, 50 Johnson & Johnson, 100 International Harvester." All solid, typical trust department stocks. This is the best business of any for a stockbroker. It means merely placing the orders and collecting the commissions, virtually no work and no problems. Best of all, someone *else* makes the decision about what to buy and sell.

I want to begin to answer some of the questions about institutional money management: how do you get this business and how good are *their* decisions? I also want to discuss how you, the average investor, can take advantage of information supposedly only privy to the account with half a million dollars or more.

Let me split the institutions for now into two sections: a) trust departments of banks and b) mutual funds with management divisions who counsel, for a fee, large broker-age accounts.

I am convinced that most people go to trust departments for safety of their principal and for bookkeeping facilities. Generally the banks' performance leaves a lot to be desired. Banks are conservative; they are unwieldy; they can be incredibly inefficient. Until recently they have had to make do with many second-rate people as analysts and as trust officers. Why is this? Simply because qualified younger people interested in money management gravitate to better-paying jobs (banks are still notoriously stingy), and more important, they gravitate to the places where aggressive people can get a piece of the action. Everyone is interested in equity today for the reason that it is impossible to get rich on a salary. No matter how much you make in ordinary income, either you spend it or it's taxed.

Staffed with lawyers who don't practice law, analysts who washed out of brokerage firms, low-pressure thinkers who like the tick of pocket watches and the solidity of seeing college classmates, trust departments move with a checklist of Approved Stocks that has been around since the United Fruit Company had its Great White Fleet.

"There was a revolution in the trust departments in the middle 1960's, and the banks lost billions of dollars in accounts when the Performance Cult hit Wall Street. One of the first orders I received as a broker was from a trust company, to buy 300 U.S. Steel at 97¼. It is now around 30 and still on the approved list. My buy order was eleven years ago, and it's been downhill ever since.

"We're expecting a recovery in the steels this year," say bulletins from the bank. And when I question the trust officer about this now (he's still at the bank, naturally) he says, "Big Steel was a solid company then; she's a solid company now. Good as gold. The trust department has seen 'em come and g ɔ. We'll stick with quality."

The clue here is that he referred to U.S. Steel as "she"; like a ship Well, the ship has not sunk, but the Staten Island Ferry has been a better bargain in the last decade than Big Steel. As for investment people who refer to stocks as "she" . . . Bella Abzug better not get caught in the cobwebs of some trust departments I know about.

When the Performance Cult really got moving in 1966 and stocks were doubling and tripling in five and six months, trust department–approved lists of high-grade issues would be up a point, down a half, on average. Customers would call and say, "*What* are you doing in Telephone and Pacific Lighting and Ford, for God's sake? *Tenneco* to you is a speculative issue. Loew's Theatres you never even heard of. What is my mother's million and a half, rest her soul, doing in your bank? Last quarter you're up 4 per cent for our portfolio. I can get 5 per cent standing on my head in a daily-interest account. Wake up!"

This attitude angered and confused the trust departments, and they shuffled their personnel, watching accounts being transferred to brokerage houses and other money managers as rapidly as winos draining jugs of California Sauterne. I have a list from 1965 of stocks bought through me by one of the most reputed trust departments in the country. The list includes El Paso Natural Gas at 24 (now 18 after six years); Anaconda at 43 (now 20); Telephone at 68½ (now 44); General Motors at 105 (now 68). This is just a sampling. And these stocks are not just in a decline *this* year; they've been losing money for people for a long time. The same stocks are *still* on the bank's approved list, and the posture they take is that it doesn't matter where they buy their favored stocks. Eventually they'll be proven correct. After all, they point out, they're a Fiduciary. It's true that they are a fiduciary and eventually they may be proven correct. But there are an awful lot of people today who would like to enjoy profits and an occasional capital gain in their own lifetimes.

There are too many committees who must pass on investment selection to make trust departments anything but unwieldy. And there are other cute tricks I've seen over the years, some methods of bank trading departments staffed by the clerks and salaried employees who enter and often direct the orders on their own discretion.

One day a few years ago, the head trader at one of the big city banks came in to see me. We had chatted on the phone a great deal and I had half a dozen sizable clients at the bank who wanted their pension business placed through me.

"I always wanted to meet you in person," the head trader said. He looked respectable, had been on the trading desk at the trust department for some years and wielded a great deal of authority. "You know I wield a great deal of authority at the bank," he went on. "On many orders that I place every day I have total decision as to which broker receives them." (This is true at every trust department's order room, too, incidentally.)

"Yes," I said, "you've been very kind. I know I've gotten every order directed to me that I'm supposed to." (This is a sticky area. Often a client will specify that *you* get the business, and the bank ignores the instructions or pretends to have lost them.)

"I'm in a little bit of a jam," the trader said. "Frankly, I need a loan to get over the Christmas season and I'm told you are such a sympathetic, discreet person you could be of help."

I was amazed at the request and initially believed he needed help. "How much would do it?" I asked.

"A hundred I need," he said. "But fifty would tide me over. I could pay you back in a few weeks."

I gave him $50 and thought it was the strangest touch I had ever had. That afternoon he called me to buy 100 Corn Products (now CPC International) and 100 American Hospital Supply.

"These aren't directed," he told me. "These are from me by way of thanks."

I immediately called a friend who is a big broker around town. "Kiss the fifty good-bye," he said. "That was no loan. Don't you know how they operate? It's a kickback. The fund traders do it, banks, trading rooms with the little old ladies in the insurance companies. It's never much, a few hundred here or there. Sometimes even lunches with wine and the whole bit. It makes them feel that they're part of the system. Just burn the canceled check when you get it back."

I felt that someone had taken infrared shots of me in the nude with Linda Christian when I was supposed to be out selling mutual funds. I was tainted. My fiduciary cover was blown.

Moral dilemmas should be resolved immediately. Once you let them drag on, not only does a solution become impossible but you feel irrevocably involved as an accomplice. I buried the $50 check in my subconscious and thought it a cheap lesson. But I am glad to report I didn't get the hint, for no more loan requests ever arrived and it became a real job to keep track of all the business that was *supposed* to be directed to me from that bank.

If you have a pension plan *or* a personal inheritance *or* a great deal of money that you've married and you want trust department management, find a stockbroker with a brain to shop around with you. *Let* yourself be romanced by the banks. They need you much more than you need them. When you've made a connection, probe beneath the surface. Ask them *their* investment philosophy. Find out how often they review *your* stocks and where they get their information. Ask them specifically *who* will manage your account, and question his qualifications.

Be a boor if necessary. Say something like "If you're so smart, why aren't you rich?" When you get someone who answers that he *is* rich, you're a lot closer to someone who will do a good job for you.

Why be a nuisance or a boor? Because in a society where obtaining service of any sort is increasingly a problem, one *sure* way to get it is to establish yourself as a personality. Good guys with $1 million who are easy to get along with get taken care of *last* by money managers. *You have got to be hard-nosed to get service. There is nothing like a little fear to increase performance.*

The fear concept also applies to other institutions that will manage your money for a healthy fee (typically, 2 per cent of the asset value up to $150,000 and 1 per cent over that, annually). These institutions try to bully you the way Gucci does when you go there to buy a pair of shoes. Gucci is doing you a favor just letting you into the shop and they really think that for you Hush Puppies are the answer. The investment advisory services and the larger people — the mutual funds who have management affiliates — claim to have limits on the size of accounts they will manage. A half a million or more is standard, although these days I'm sure they won't sneeze at a $150,000 middle-class small-timer. Usually a team goes to work on you: one older, more responsible type who's seen it all since *his* father took the deep six back in '31; and two terribly attractive boy wonders who look and act the way you've always wanted to. They give you the pitch about performance and professional management, and when they leave, you've not only signed up your pension fund *and* your personal portfolio, but you wish, wistfully, that you could be so clean and efficient, and that they'd ask you to a party at *their* house or *their* club. One of the bright, scrubbed young men will be *your* personal portfolio manager. His name is Jim Jenkins. "Please don't call us," he tells you. "We'll let you know quarterly how you are doing. But we must have complete discretion. Details and small annoyances keep us from our job of superior research and performance. We must be isolated to operate."

You begin to get confirmation slips showing you've bought companies you never heard of, but you feel reassured because you're told that no money is made today in companies that anyone has heard of. Some of the companies you cannot find quoted in the paper, so you call a broker, who checks the over-the-counter pink sheets for you and you discover that everything you bought is up. Some of the stocks are *way* up. Your first quarterly accounting shows your portfolio has increased 35 per cent, but all the stocks listed seem to have the wrong prices beside them, and *some* of the stocks listed, you know you don't even own. You call Jim Jenkins.

"I'm sorry, but Mr. Jenkins is no longer with us. Your portfolio manager is now Mr. John Boyne. He's a *vice-president*." You are reassured.

"I was going to introduce myself before," said John Boyne, "but you know our policy of not being bothered in our research."

"What happened to Jim Jenkins?"

"I imagine there were differences of opinion," he says. "But you should be pleased with the performance."

"I'm thrilled," you say. "But this evaluation shows somebody else's stocks. Not mine."

Silence. Then. "Oh? Let me get the file." Pause. "I'm terribly sorry; these secretaries. You shall receive a corrected copy within the next week."

You get a corrected copy in six weeks that still is not right. But it's closer than it was and, what-the-hell, the stocks you *do* own are going through the roof.

Suddenly there seems to be a deterioration in some of your stocks. Electronic Memories has slipped 12 points; Teledyne is down 10; for a few over-the-counter beauties you cannot even find quotations. You call John Boyne, only to find that he has gone to start his own advisory service and off-shore mutual fund and now operates from Geneva. "Our *senior* vice-president, Mr. Gordon, is now handling your account," you are told.

"Mr. Gordon," you say, when you reach him. "I realize your rule on calling, but I had a $40,000 profit on National Student Marketing. What has happened?"

"Do you own *that* one?" he says. "I'm afraid that in the confusion of Mr. Boyne's leaving, he neglected to have that recorded on your list."

"Kindly close my account," you say, beginning to think that the approved list at the trust department is looking mighty good. At least you can count on the list and the same people to be around for the next hundred years. And they will be always willing to talk. You swear that the next person you meet who makes you feel embarrassed at having only a quarter of a million dollars you will kick in the crotch.

One eager young money manager, who handled smaller accounts ($50,000 and up), fell so in love with *one* company that he indirectly became the fourth-largest stockholder of it. By virtue of the fact that all his accounts were in the stock. Blinded by management's predictions which never came true, he bought for *everyone* in the low 30's and the stock fell rapidly to 12, then to 3, burying his accounts and finishing his own management company. In a manic fit and having lost most of his self-control, he sent an extraordinary letter to every customer, begging them to stay with him because "we have all learned lessons from this experience," the letter said, "and we can all profit in the future from them. I was blinded by my early success. Remember it?"

Most people may be suckers, but they don't stay fools for very long. If a money manager even *hints* at asking forgiveness for a mistake, part company by return mail. You have plenty of time for emotions and the study of them in your home; you have *no* time for sentiment when it comes to dollars and cents. The most important area in money management is continuity. You *must* be sure that whoever handles your money is happy in his work, and that he's going to be around for the long haul, not the short buck.

Thursday, July 23:

There is enthusiasm but still very slow volume. According to the SEC testimony of Mrs. Wilma Soss, a frequent gadfly at annual meetings, "the brokerage industry was broke after the longest Bull market in history." This is virtually true. I get calls every day from customers wanting their stocks shipped out to them.

I dropped in to see the resident partner, who managed a smile about the situation. "I see where Little Orphan Annie will be forty-six next week," he said. "I wish I looked half as well as she does."

It was terribly quiet. We had done a total of $175 in gross commissions in the entire office the day before. "Two years ago," the partner said, "the American Stock Exchange was doing 6 and 7 million shares a day. Now they're trading 1½ million. The stocks were selling then at $18 to $20 on average; now they're 4 and 5. No wonder income is down so much. Everyone forgets about the action on the American Exchange. We've chopped 25 per cent of our staff and so have most other big firms. But we've got to chop further until we can show a profit. I tell you, there's no feeling like working all your life for something, to see it disappear in a year. My capital is all gone."

The New York Stock Exchange Rule 325 specifies that a member firm's aggregate indebtedness must not exceed twenty times its liquid capital. Privately, the exchange has contacted all member firms, forcing them to bring this twenty-to-one ratio down to twelve to one. Brokerage houses can do this by raising new capital, or by acquiring subordinated lenders who will put up securities that the exchange will value by the "haircut" method. The method works this way: you lend a brokerage company 1,000 shares of stock worth approximately $100,000 at current market prices. The exchange gives it a value of $70,000 only — a "haircut" — saying that if liquidation of the stock were forced and dumping occurred, the value of the 1,000 shares would probably be knocked down to $70,000. The stock exchange likes to think it takes no chances.

Many potential lenders approached by brokers have taken a dim view of all this. "Who the hell is going to loan money *or* stocks to a losing business proposition?" they ask. "I've got troubles of my own." Without the public knowing the extent of the crisis, dozens of Wall Street firms were ordered to come up with new capital or be forced into liquidation. Donaldson, Lufkin and Jenrette, the first brokerage house to go public (at 15) was 7⅝ by August 7. On August 10 Dempsey-Tegeler was forced into closing, and rumors were that they would require $9 to $15 *million* to protect their customers. The special trust fund of the New York Stock Exchange would not be nearly enough to bail out the many firms rumored to be in trouble.

McDonnell and Company had closed in March after

sixty-five years in business, and on August 18, First Devonshire and Charles ("Two-a-week Charlie") Plohn were suspended by the exchange. IBM was a new low at 227, and
although most blue-chip stocks had substantial recoveries
in the last month, the brokers in my office were not averaging $50 a week net. And had not been for some time.
Ten Big Board firms are facing liquidation or are liquidated, and major firms with thousands of clients —
Hayden, Stone; Goodbody; F. I. duPont — are in big
trouble. Southern California alone has had eight companies go under in the last three months. (This is not really
surprising if you've ever been to Southern California.)
Customers all over the country have their securities and
their money frozen, with no *real* guarantees that they will
ever receive them back. Hayden, Stone has suits against
them from customers totalling almost *$7 million.*

Friday, August 21:

I have just received a memo from Eaton and Howard (a
large mutual fund complex) raising commission rates on
their income fund to 8 per cent. Their brochure has a
sunny face printed on it with the legend *Keep smiling.* Carl
Yastrzemski works for Eaton and Howard. His batting
average is only four hundred points below the Dow.

I got a call from a friend who told me that a broker we
both knew had been found in a motel last night. Dead.
"Shot himself," I was told. "Had that big house and four
kids and he wasn't able to make a living. Stuck a pistol
right into his mouth and blew off the top of his head." I
can remember forcing myself to believe that this had all

happened before, and thinking that inventories are very small in the stores; that consumer demand is the key to the fall and to next year. I began to buy retail and discount department store stocks: Allied Stores at 23; May Department Stores at 19½; King's Department Stores at 15.

Where did everything go wrong? I kept thinking. And what can I do about it?

In the 1960's we had been in an industry geared strictly to writing orders. Orders without real controls behind them of any kind. In the control area, few studies of the problems in brokerage firms ever discuss the "fail" situation. When a brokerage firm tries to reconcile the securities they can physically lay their hands on against what shows in the customers' accounts and they find 50,000 shares of General Motors missing — that's a fail situation. The term means that a brokerage house *fails to show* securities that are listed in its customers' accounts. It could mean that the broker has *failed to receive* certificates from a customer or another broker who owes them securities. Or it could mean that the broker has *failed to find* the stock; it could be lost, stolen or misplaced.

One of the factors that has been driving our resident partner wild is that a year ago my own firm had *millions* of dollars in such fails — several million dollars worth of stock that we owed to customers and that we could not put our hands on. If you are in a partnership, *everything* can be attached by people who want to sue you: automobiles, homes, Duncan Phyfe chairs, color televisions. You are going to witness, next year, the largest scurry to incorporate on the part of firms in an industry in the history of the United States. And don't let your broker kid you by saying it's to pave the way for firms eventually going public or selling out. It's primarily to save the skins of the members of the firm. No one likes trucks driving up to their suburban homes with movers carrying out furniture to warehouses for auction.

One main reason for this fail rate has been bookkeeping. Record keeping was abominable in the back offices on Wall Street, and although the partners cared, no one who worked as a clerk or keypunch operator gave a damn. I had a customer come to me at the beginning of 1969 from Hayden, Stone who said they had delivered to him 100 shares of Mobil Oil that he didn't own. Five thousand dollars' worth of stock. "I sent it back," he explained, "saying I didn't own it. They delivered it to me again. Again I sent it back and, can you believe, they delivered another 100 shares four weeks later? So, I'm an honest guy, but evidently they couldn't find where it belonged. I brought the Mobil to the bank and took a loan on it. *I* might as well use the money; people don't drop five grand in your lap every day." Multiply this incident by thousands of similar ones and there was probably over $1 billion worth of securities the industry could not account for.

One firm worked night and day and weekends for months, finding the multimillion dollars' worth of stock that was missing. Certificates turned up everywhere: stuffed behind pipes in ladies' rooms, at the bottoms of trash baskets, in the backs of filing cabinets with old letters. One thousand Consolidated Edison turned up in a drawerful of *Wall Street Journals* from 1957. You can begin to see why people with new capital were reluctant to come to the aid of the industry.

At this point, we have our house almost in order operationally. We are down in fails from many millions to a few hundred thousand, a pittance that will probably turn up somewhere in the research department. The other major Wall Street firms are also in vastly improved shape. All that is needed now is some business. Everyone is hoping that reform has not come too late and that not many of these stories will come to light. I would suggest, *if* you are a *long-term* investor, that you have your brokerage firm send out your stocks or bonds to you as you purchase them. If delivery takes more than four weeks, call your broker *every day* until he gets you some satisfaction. When the day comes that you can do business with your present stockbroker *for one year* without incident, with every confirmation and monthly statement correct, with every certificate and dividend received on time, with every check mailed on the due date, *then* you can bring back your stocks to him for safekeeping. Only then can you be sure that he has cleaned house and that there will be no surprises at the bottom of the trash baskets of Wall Street.

The last week in August:

On continuing rumors about easing of interest rates and a possible cut in the prime, the market has been strong and volume is increasing. My Cenco Instruments is up to 32¼ (although I kissed it good-bye at 29⅞ as planned) and retail stocks have been very strong.

Georgie the Pill, sitting in the front of the boardroom, is buying Polaroid at 71 in 1,000-share lots. "Fears of a liquidity crisis have faded," he reads to everyone from the

Wall Street Journal. "The Bear market is over," he exults, thrilled to see activity on the tape. His enthusiasm gets the registered reps busy on the phones. With 13-, 14-, 15-million-share days and the barrier of Labor Day about to be crossed, people can begin feeling good about the autumn.

"Hey, Georgie," Jim Curran yelled out. "Did you read the other day that doctors say Beethoven's deafness was definitely *not* caused by syphilis?"

Georgie was watching the tape for his Polaroid trades to pass. "Beethoven," he said, smiling for the first time in months, "wasn't he an institutional man for First Devonshire?"

7.

The Sensuous Broker

It is difficult, if not impossible, to separate getting involved with people's money from getting involved in people's lives. People are extreme in their opinions about who should handle money and how to handle money. And they are extreme in their opinions about how to live their lives. But it all hangs out on the closely printed pages of prices on the stock exchanges. Discussing those prices, where else can people get a sounding board, a sympathetic ear for conversation that is not cut off after forty-five minutes by the shrink? The difference between an analyst's couch and the stockbroker's office is that the analysts hear all the fantasies. We get the realities.

The most avid followers of the market who are female fall into two categories: widows with deep longings, or un-

happily married women with deep longings. Divorcées
generally have no time for fascination with trading stocks
or commodities; they're too busy lining up baby-sitters or
beefing up the alimony or creating their new images. Which
is fine. But widows, in their own opinion, have the money
and the time and the experience that comes with maturity
to be great traders. They have had the will and the good
fortune to outlive their husbands; certainly they should
have the will and the good fortune to succeed in the stock
market. The unhappy wives have just as much determina-
tion. They are preparing themselves for their eventual roles
as widows, and since many are unable to have affairs, they
substitute the romance of money for the romance of a
lover's arms.

I used to have a client named Saul who had all kinds of
theories about women based on his own personal observa-
tion. At age forty-four he had sold an apartment building he owned for $1 million. He then retired. But Saul had
no hobbies, hated his wife, didn't play golf and could not
bring himself to go back to work. He even contemplated
suicide until he discovered the ticker tape and a comfortable chair next to my desk. He was the ideal customer.
He'd come in near ten-thirty in the morning, buy 100 IBM
(he ran a continuing balance of $50,000 with me), read
the *Journal, Business Week, Women's Wear Daily,* mind
his own business and go for a long lunch. In the afternoon,
he'd fall asleep in his chair, snore a bit (which was not a
great advertisement for my office, but he did trade every
day) and wake up eventually, in time to sell his IBM. Some
days he'd make a few bucks, $200 or so; some days he'd
lose two or three hundred. But *every* day he generated

$150 in commissions, a meal ticket for me. This gave him the right to be a philosopher, and it gave him a home.

"Women will drive you bananas, kid," he'd tell me. "You know something? Everyone talks about sex, but no one does anything about it. I learned years ago that wives just want to be left alone. Give them a checking account and don't get in their way. So I decided not to get in their way. Don't get married, kid, they'll tear the heart out of you."

Saul was disgusted with me for having women customers, and when one would visit the office, he'd go for a walk, coming back when the coast was clear.

After a time, things deteriorated domestically for Saul and he became increasingly abusive in his lessons to me.

"They'll break your hump, kid," he'd say. "When you deal with women's money they're nothing but poison. Put the IBM in at 247½."

After Saul had been a client for about a year, he decided to go to Phoenix for the winter sun. Just for a week to get away from his wife. They often took separate vacations, which suited them both just fine. It's been three years and Saul is still in Phoenix. He tried calling me long-distance at first to trade IBM but he needed the ambience of a broker's office. One day he said, "Look, I can lose money in Phoenix without the long-distance calls. You're a good kid but you never learned a lesson. You got to learn to take advice — don't let the women break your hump. You got an enemy who's a broker? Send the women to him."

Some time later he sent me a box of pecans and a copy of *Arizona Highways* with "Best Wishes" scrawled across the cover. The pictures were very nice and I guessed it was his way of saying that there were no hard feelings.

One solution for handling female accounts was given me by an older broker who used to take me to lunch when I was training in New York. He'd have two martinis, a big bowl of Manhattan clam chowder and he'd tell me to beware of women customers.

"Men are impossible and stupid," he told me. "And the richer they are, in most cases, the stupider. But women are crazy. When their goddamn metabolisms are controlled by the phases of the moon, which they are, you know you're not dealing with anything rational. I sell *all* my lady customers Tampax stock. No one ever asks me what the company does; no one ever asks me about the future for it. It's a beautiful gimmick; it puts them off-balance when I recommend it. I sell them out of everything else, buy them Tampax, ship out the stock and kiss them goodbye. They always make money because the stock keeps going up, pardon the expression, and you dispense with any conversation. Promise them anything, but give them Tampax. Some more chowder?"

Tuesday, September 8:

Since I've been in the brokerage business, I've had dealings with hundreds of women and I've learned that they love to be involved with their stockbroker. Some deeper than others. I received a call this morning from Mike the film distributor, an amusing customer who is always inviting me to his office to preview sixteen-millimeter skin flicks that he's trying to get launched in this city. PORN AND POP-CORN, reads a plaque on his desk. Another reads TO THE WALL WITH CENSORSHIP.

"What's hot?" he asked me.

"I should be asking you."

"Christ," he said. "This town is incredible. I'm getting shut down all over the city."

"What do you think of Twentieth Century–Fox?" I asked him.

"Forget it. Fox is just a showcase for Zanuck's broads now. Red ink all over the place. United Artists (a division now of TransAmerica) and Columbia are the only film companies I trust."

"What about MGM?"

"Jim Aubrey can have as many auctions as he wants. He can sell off every pair of Judy Garland's shoes and they're still in trouble. The only way to save MGM is to reissue *Gone With the Wind, 2001,* and *The Wizard of Oz* over and over and over. Every time they make anything new, it's a bomb."

"Jim Aubrey is a hero of mine," I told Mike the film distributor.

"I won't talk films with amateurs," he decided. "What arouses you is *Bambi*." He rang off.

Jim Aubrey, the "Smiling Cobra," had been brought in by Kirk Kekorian to run MGM and turn it around. For years I had read about Aubrey, his success as president of CBS Television, his cold-hearted reputation and especially his triumphs with women. Aubrey was celebrated for something I read about and that I came to call the Jim Aubrey Lunch, or How to Dispose of a Woman Gracefully. Aubrey, handsome and supposedly cruel, would call a woman whom he was tired of and invite her to luncheon at Pavillon, or La Côte Basque, or "21." He'd give her cocktails, wine, a four-course meal, topped off by coffee and perhaps some brandy. As she basked in his attention, lulled by the food and drink and fawning service, Aubrey would tell her good-bye and, in the words he was quoted as saying, "walk out into the sunshine a free man." The lady, who could never make a scene at La Côte Basque, would presumably dab at a tear, have another brandy and vanish from Aubrey's life. I thought the Jim Aubrey Lunch was terribly fine and I longed to carry off something like it.

A year after I read the article, I was handling the account of an amorous widow, wealthy enough to indulge herself without worry, but still very interested in capital gains. As who isn't? Her husband had been a lawyer specializing in maritime cases. He was killed in the crash of a Grumman Goose on his way from Guantanamo to Miami. She had wanted him so badly when they were in college together that she forced herself to stay in the background after they were married, subordinating their life to his career. After his death, as she told me later, "The *real* I emerged." The lawyer had planned his estate well. The widow and two children inherited almost $2 million, $750,000 of it in securities, mostly blue-chip stocks and bonds. These she promptly sold and began to take large positions in stocks she had researched; this research consisting of following tips from successful former friends of her husband. She bought 3,000 American Zinc at 35, within a point of its all-time high, and rode it to 25 before selling. It is now 7½. But then Scan Data is 5 (it was

180) and Liquidonics is 10 (it was 170). She owned them both and took big losses. They had both been recommendations of a friend of her husband's.

"Maybe they were not as good friends as you think," I told her.

"Charlie Simpson was his college roommate," she said (Charlie had given her Liquidonics at 150). "He worshipped my husband. And he told me he'd give me information for life if I'd go to bed with him. Friends are like that."

"If you want to go to bed with him," I said, "I would suggest taking jewelry or furs. Let him keep his information."

"That's just like something my husband would say," she said, looking differently at me for the first time.

"Suddenly I feel like I'm a girl again," she told me after a while, and I thought I had heard the line before. She began wearing knee socks and letting her hair grow long and she bought fun furs and read *Steppenwolf* and *Cat's Cradle*. And she began to let me recoup her losses, relying less and less upon what she was calling "old men's ideas" and more upon my suggestions. There were fringe benefits to the charade also, great Christmas presents (Turnbull and Asser monogrammed shirts), great birthday presents (a first-edition David Copperfield), weekly mercy errands for me to laundry and cleaners. But after a year and a half, during which time we made big hits in Stanley Works, KLM, and Diners Club, she began to haunt my apartment, waiting for me to get home from dates. I would find her asleep in her station wagon in her fun fur and long boots, a transistor radio pathetically tuned in to a rock station. I rationalized the situation by telling myself that I was the stockbroker for all seasons; that without my honest approach to her money, she would have it plucked from her. I represented, in my mind, the sole defense she had from predatory con men. But when her behavior became hysterical concerning my social life, and when Benjy our order clerk began to whistle "Just a Gigolo" when she brought me my morning coffee and Danish in the office, I decided it was time for the Jim Aubrey Lunch. I was beginning to imagine headlines: BIG PRODUCER SHOT TO DEATH IN OFFICE, or CUSTOMER GETS EVEN WITH CUSTOMER'S MAN; RELEASED ON JUSTIFIABLE HOMICIDE. Even a three-quarter-of-a-million-dollar account was not worth the aggravation. Not to mention the fear, I thought, slipping my silver cuff links (another present) into my Turnbull and Asser cuffs. Feeling relieved, and determined to part friends if possible, I decided to tell her to take her account to Fiduciary Trust or someone like that, who would dole out money to her on a scheduled basis, increasing the yield and preserving her capital.

We met at the finest luncheon spot in the city and each had two Tanqueray Gibsons on the rocks. I complimented her on how she looked, dressed to the nines with newly streaked hair and a Chanel suit. We had littlenecks, small salads and marvelously fresh sole with a '66 Blanc de Leparon. She wanted café diablo and I obliged. The sun was shining and I knew I would walk out into it a free man, just like Jim Aubrey. When she had her first sip, I told her that she was one of the finest people I had ever known but that it was all over. "You're going to have to take your account elsewhere. I can no longer serve you properly."

In the finest restaurant in the city, at the height of the lunch hour, on the busiest day of the week, she started to scream at the top of her voice. Not words. Just scream sounds. The maître d' rushed over. Waiters rushed over. She would not stop. "I'm only kidding," I blurted out. "I'm not serious. A little joke."

Lunch cost me $32 including the café diablo and I was still stuck. She insisted on buying 500 Technical Operations to salve the embarrassment and I realized that I was going to have to look for a hero other than Jim Aubrey. What would *he* have done when the screaming started? I'll never know, but the Jim Aubrey Lunch as a viable concept was dead. I had forgotten to figure the money angle. As a matter of pure emotion, I might have gotten away without a scene. But with $750,000 in stocks sitting in a box on Wall Street in *our* firm's name, my widow felt entitled to hysteria. I should have known there was a dimension I had overlooked.

She began to be wary after that, suspicious whenever she bought a stock that I recommended and it went down half a point. Sensing the end, she began to trade in a frenzy, calling me from phone booths on her way into town because she couldn't wait to buy something. I finally blew up in my office. "For God's sake," I asked her. "What do you think I am, a money-making screwing machine?"

She stomped out in a huff to Bonwit's.

Lacking the courage to tell her good-bye for a second time, I did the next-best thing: I unloaded her on a doctor. Even better than an ordinary doctor — a surgeon. The world's most expert person on every subject. Especially investments. He gave her the benefit of his experience, leveraging her up to the ears in convertible bonds, which he got her to hock at a bank, so she could come back with the money and buy *more* convertible bonds on margin (putting up only 50 per cent of the purchase price). As she warmed to him, she cooled to me, which my mother always told me is the way of the world. One day she came into the office with her hair cut off and done in the blown up Puff Adder style so popular in the middle 1960's. She wore stockings and David Evins pumps and had shed her Briarcliff-skirt-and-sweater for something that looked like she was about to be photographed as a sponsor for a Charity Ball.

"I should like it if you would ship out my securities to me please," she said formally.

"You didn't like the café diablo," I said, trying to tease her out of the inevitable. She didn't crack.

"David will be handling my affairs now." (David was the surgeon; she blushed slightly.) "Nothing personal," she added, turning on her well-wrought heels and walking out, her 750K portfolio wagging its tail behind her.

Benjy the order clerk saw her leave and leaned over the trading counter, grinning at me. "They don't yell; they don't tell; they don't swell," he said, "and they're grateful as hell."

Jim Aubrey would have fired him. I went out for a corned-beef sandwich. Lean.

Being in a *people* business, not a *thing* business, there is a constant danger to the broker of carrying these people too far, in getting too involved with their personal lives. If you are an investor, on the other hand, I would much rather see you become involved with your stockbroker than with your stocks. Your broker can become a known quantity. Remember that. But those little pieces of paper, the stock certificates, with the naked, buxom ladies on them, will always be a mystery to you. Never forget it.

As for these personal relationships, one story I will tell you is about my client named Sandy who was a virtuoso drummer when he was a kid. "The best feet since Elvin Jones," everybody said, and feet are very important for a drummer. Buddy Rich approved of him; he thought Sandy had it all. My client was playing in Vegas when he was twenty-two years old, solos that had people tapping on their whiskey sour glasses with spoons. One night, one of the biggest druggists in the country walked in with his wife and sixteen-year-old daughter. He owned twenty-three drugstores in the Twin Cities area. The daughter was not only beautiful, she had a thing for drummers. Sandy smelled money and he saw that the girl was beautiful and he married her a year later. But his quick feet and quick hands left him at age twenty-four; he couldn't keep time to a two-step. It was all gone.

Sandy retreated, with his bride, to his family business, manufacturing ironing-board covers. She felt cheated, but her father, a large stock market operator as well as druggist, did not want her back in St. Paul. A divorce would be a disgrace to her father's name; and his name adorned twenty-three drugstores. Sandy's wife went to a psychiatrist and stayed with the marriage. But one afternoon she came home from shopping and cut all of Sandy's neckties off at half mast. Another day she drove her brand-new Thunderbird smack into Sandy's Toronado, which was parked in their garage. She had a nervous breakdown, went back to the Twin Cities, was urged to return to her husband and did.

Hating the ironing-board-cover business and anxiously waiting for his father-in-law to die, Sandy fell into Mitty-like fantasy, believing himself to be a stock market trader of immense proportions. He would call me four or five times a day from phone booths and diners and the offices of his customers. He *had* to know every eighth of a point change, every share traded, not only for his own small portfolio ($6,000 or $7,000) but for every stock of his father-in-law. These quote sessions could take five minutes apiece, cheap enough therapy for him, even at thirty cents a call. But he turned over his $6,000 or $7,000 at least weekly, not able to sit in a stock. (If *you* called your broker five times a day, *you* wouldn't be able to sit in a stock, either.)

For a while he was one of my biggest customers, in terms of commission business, because he was in and out of his position so often. And because of this activity he felt himself entitled to a little romance — his broker should take him out for dinner once in a while. Him *and* his wife. Once a year we had the mandatory shrimp cocktail, the expense-account steak au poivre and crêpes suzettes. On one of these command-performance dinners, where I would arrive early and have many drinks, his beautiful wife who had been wild for drummers started drumming her fingers on my thigh. This has a way of changing the dimensions of a customer-broker relationship. When Sandy excused himself to the men's room after his second Planter's Punch, she grabbed my hand. "He's such a pig," she said. "He disgusts me. I make him shave at the factory before he comes home every night. I make him have manicures."

"How can you stay married?" I asked, rubbing my thumb along the back of her hand, "if you make each other so miserable?"

"He's sick," she said. "But we don't know anyone. I have no friends; he has no friends. Just this crap about the stock market and being a *big* man. His only friends are the financial pages. The funny thing is that he doesn't even know what he's reading. My father calls every Saturday at five-thirty and chews him out for being an idiot."

Sandy came back slurring his words and her hand again dropped to my thigh.

"You know I traded *$1 million* worth of stock last year," were the first words he said. "It took me four hours to prepare my buy and sell slips for the accountant."

"Why don't you die?" his wife said softly, staring vacantly at her crème caramel which Sandy had made her order.

I was glad we only had to do this once a year.

Whenever he called me in the office, Sandy never mentioned his ironing-board covers. He never mentioned his wife or children or his friends or their social life. His relationship with me was one-dimensional: give him quotations, good service, and eventually his father-in-law would die and make Sandy my biggest account.

Sometime after the obligatory dinner, Sandy's wife went into intensive analysis and he began calling me *six* times a day for prices. By this time he had traded himself into the ground, losing half of his original capital, and was determined to sit on *one* stock until he could recoup. I felt

I was at the siege of Stalingrad, *inside* the city. He'd fire away with phone calls for quotations. But no business. I didn't have the heart to tell him good-bye; I could see him making the rounds of other brokerage offices with his sad routine, and I decided to keep his flame of self-delusion alive.

But I began having my secretary give him the quotations four of the six times he called.

"What are you, some kind of big shot?" he'd say when I finally talked with him.

"Look, Sandy. I don't have the time to give quotes all day. The market is only open so many hours."

"Some day it'll be all worth it," he'd say. "We've learned a lot together."

"You ain't just whistling 'Dixie,' " I said. He would be lucky if his wife restricted her scissors work to his neckties.

A month later *she* called me. "I've got to see you," she said.

I've always taken people to their illogical conclusions and I couldn't say no. I told her to meet me for lunch, choosing someplace dark. But it wasn't dark enough. She had gained at least seventeen pounds; she wore a long, dark, shapeless dress (before the midi) to hide her weight, but it only served to make her look grotesque. She could not keep her eyes on anything for more than ten seconds without nervously casting about. Her first drink, a Bloody Mary, she spilled in my lap.

"Sandy is going to have to turn over *two* million dollars next year," I said to her. "Bloody Mary stays forever."

She was too eager to towel me off and I was wishing I were back in my nice safe office next to my nice, warm

Bunker-Ramo machine giving her husband all the quotations he wanted.

"Let's take a room somewhere," she blurted out. "I'll pay for it. I just want to be held."

"It's time to go," I told her. "I'm just not equipped to handle this sort of —"

With that she began tugging at the tablecloth, threatening to put my chicken croquettes in my lap, Supreme Sauce and all, on top of the Bloody Mary.

"It's the frigging stock market," she said, sobbing. "I just want to be held and not hear about Douglas Aircraft and General Dynamics and American frigging Standard. I could puke with all that stuff."

"People get emotional about their stocks," I told her, pulling the tablecloth in the opposite direction. "Sandy is a good guy."

"Sandy is an idiot," she said. "All my father ever talked about was stocks, all my husband ever talks about is stocks. *You never* talk about stocks."

"That's because I'm a broker."

"Just hold me," she said. "Leave Sandy to his ironing-board covers. Let him pull one over his head."

I threw money onto the table and, in a cold sweat, talked her into a cab, first making her promise she would go directly to her doctor.

Falling into my swivel chair, I swore that never again would I become involved. It was two o'clock. At three o'clock, Sandy's wife called, or rather the man who owned the hardware store two doors from my office called.

"I've got a crazy broad here asking for you," he said. "I've called the cops."

"I'm off to sell a mutual fund," I told my secretary and rushed out to find Sandy's wife in shock, in the power tool department. I was terrified.

"I'm just a dirty piece of ice," she babbled incoherently. "I'm just a dirty piece of ice."

It shivered my timbers.

Between grabs for the door handle and threats of suicide on her part, I managed to drive her home. Then I called Sandy and explained the situation. He said he'd come right home. "Did you happen to see the last on General Dynamics before you left the office?" he asked me just as he hung up. Why hadn't I gone to medical school?

Since then I have not had to undergo another command-performance dinner. Sandy still does not trade actively, still calls four times a day for *his* prices *and* his father-in-law's prices, and he is my sixth circle of hell. I feel that only me and my magic quote machine are keeping him from insanity, and I stay with the job. But my idea of eternal damnation is a brokerage office with an endlessly moving ticker tape and no one calling but Sandy, who endlessly asks for quotations and never places an order. He never mentions his wife to me and I only ask after *her* at Christmas and New Year's. Our relationship is cordial and every month he reminds me of how things are going to be when his father-in-law goes to the Happy Hunting Ground. His father-in-law will outlive us all.

Part of the American Dream is to make the Big Score by accident, to make it overnight with an inheritance, a marriage, or a master scheme that does it for you with very little work. I have had countless customers who have thought they could do it in the stock market, while they continued to live the Good Life.

Paul Benedict believed in this American Dream, although he hadn't married it and would not inherit it. When he opened his account with me he said, "I don't want to be lectured and I don't want any of your ideas. You just get me good execution of orders and pay me on time and I'll be grateful. I do my own hunting for ideas."

To say that Benedict liked action was like saying Wimpy liked hamburgers. He would bet on anything: horses, dogs, trotters, cards. On every sporting event and side bets within the event, how many hits Tony Oliva would get against Washington, how many penalties Keith Magnuson would get against the St. Louis Blues. He also liked sex. But he liked to pay for it. "I haven't slept with my wife in five weeks," he enjoyed bragging. "But I've spent $100 a week for five weeks on twelve different babes. Now buy me 50 Computer Sciences, 50 Digital, 50 Leasco Data, 40 Xerox, 25 IBM, and 30 Disney."

"Why don't you buy *one* or *two* stocks," I would urge him. "Commissions just eat you up. You'll need a point before you break even on those things."

This was his trading method, a mad random sampling of glamour stocks bought for no particular reason and, in most cases, sold almost the next day if they didn't move. He was inevitably late paying and I was always getting him extensions of time, which is a no-no and for which you must put in requests to the stock exchange.

Paul Benedict enjoyed calling me from hotel rooms, when he'd say to me, "Sell everything out and buy 50

Muter, 50 Hess Oil, 50 Teledyne, and here's someone to say hello."

There would be a pause with his hand over the receiver, then —

"Hi. This is Gerri. How about a *good* time? We've got this big bed and Paul says you can share it."

Then Paul would get back on. "Do I know how to live, or do I know how to live?"

"You know how to live," I would tell him. "You sure you want to buy all these odd lots?"

"Just put them in," he'd say to me, "while *I* go put it in." Click.

I must say that he must have liked me because he was always trying to get his girls to open accounts and buy stocks. Robert W. Haack, the president of the New York Stock Exchange, would love that. After all, he's opposed to fixed commission rates, and who enjoys a good haggling better than the girls of the afternoon hotel rooms?

None of the girls ever did open accounts. But one nice-sounding one, who claimed she had spent two years at Smith, wanted to buy a mutual fund contractual plan, putting away $50 a month. I encouraged her to go to Switzerland and duck her money there. She said she'd consider it and that I sounded cute. But Paul was getting jealous by this time and grabbed the phone back, taking out his aggression by selling everything and buying nine odd lots. He almost never made a profit.

"You're going to bury yourself," I told him. "You can't keep trading like this. It doesn't make any sense."

"I'm trying out some theories," he told me. "When the

time comes to consolidate, we'll shoot the works. If I make two hundred grand, I'll take you to Japan with me. I've always wanted to get a babe to walk on my back. American babes are too big. They'd kill me."

Paul never got a chance for the Big Score. It turned out he had borrowed up to the ears to gamble and to play the market and there were certain boys who were about to lean on him if payment was not forthcoming. He sold all his stocks, took the proceeds, and disappeared for seven months. I ran into him in the street over a year after that. He was pushing a sample case of fabrics on the sidewalk, one of those big suitcases on wheels. He didn't smile and he didn't tell me about his women.

"I'm on the road selling now," he told me. "For my father-in-law. My pay goes to a trust account and I get a goddamn allowance. We're seeing a marriage counselor and I suppose I'm all straightened out."

"That's good, Paul," I said. "I miss you, but I know it's for the best."

"Let's get together for lunch sometime," he said. "Nothing fancy. A sandwich and a beer maybe."

"That would be fine."

"Boy, do you remember the good old days?"

I told him I did.

He began to push his case away, then looked back. "Bet you five bucks I can beat you in a foot race to the corner. Me pushing the case; you just running."

"Stockbrokers don't run," I told him.

"Yeah, it figures," he said. "Well, you always were a lousy gambler."

THE SENSUOUS BROKER

Men like their stockbrokers to know how successful they are with women. They equate adventures with money and adventures in sex. Women often use money and the stock market in quite a different way, as a club against their husbands and fathers. Stock market activity for them is always a rebellion *against* sex, a liberation from the sexual roles forced upon them by the male. This is all right with me. We get them coming and going. The men like to sprinkle anecdotes with their transactions; the women are strictly business.

I have a client who is the executive vice-president of a listed company. He has had a mistress in New York for years, and each spring he buys a few shares of his company's stock in her name.

"I don't want to give her any ideas about other companies," he would tell me. "If I bought her some General Motors or some Standard Oil, the first thing you know she gets ideas about other men. You catch? I don't want her getting ideas about other men *or* companies."

But recently he has complained to me. "I don't take the heat like I used to," he says. "I'm not interested when all she wants is more allowance, more clothes, a new apartment. But I don't know how to dump her. Can you imagine that? I make $80,000 a year and *I'm* afraid to dump *her*? Let me tell you something about a mistress. They get worse than a wife. Sometimes I wonder why I bother. Look, buy her 10 shares. Send the bill to my office and I'll bring in a cashier's check. And do me a favor. If you can think of something, a way out, let me know. Used to be that I *absolutely* lived for something strange. Now I just want to be left alone."

Randolph was a physical-fitness nut who was dedicated to keeping in shape. He also believed that if you had $100,000 you could make a living from the stock market; a few hot deals along the way would eliminate the necessity of working from nine to five with all the other poor slobs. Randolph became a client of mine by accident. Mutual friends had introduced us and I convinced him over cocktails one night that I was the best stockbroker in the business. He believed me, sending me $100,000 and following my ideas.

Independently wealthy and young, he had a wife, four children, assorted pets and unusual ideas about living his life. "I only eat two meals a day," he told me. "For lunch I had wine and two dozen oysters. Usually only twenty-three of them work. I must make love every day, lift weights, have twelve hundred milligrams of vitamin C, rose hips pills, one sixteen-ounce steak and see lots of pornography."

"In that order?" I asked him.

He would fly to New York once a week, ostensibly to "work on a deal." Actually, he would camp in the Forty-second Street stroke houses and come back with tales of what they were getting away with now. "And I saw at least five classmates there in the afternoon last week," he would tell me, "with briefcases and vests. Beautiful. At least I'm no hypocrite." And that was true.

But Randolph would always take his profits *out* of the market and let the losses sit. Eventually, it meant whittling down his principal, when he'd be forced to sell to keep up with mortgage payments, light bill and his porno habit, which was getting expensive to satisfy. Whenever you are forced to liquidate stocks, you invariably get horrible prices.

Nineteen sixty-nine and the first seven months of 1970 were getting Randolph on edge. One day he came into the office and announced that the bloodsuckers of America were bleeding him dry. He popped a rose hips into his mouth, flexed, and swallowed it without water. "I'm going to the Greek islands, to Mykonos," he told me. "A sunshine world where people are stripped to their essentials and the women wear peasant blouses. American women have no breasts. *You* run the account and send me $1,000 a month. Bill collectors are camped on my doorstep."

"You taking the family?"

"Christ," Randolph said, "would Zorba take the family? Hey," he said, lowering his voice, "you ever handle that little number?" He pointed to the girl assistant on the order desk.

I gave him a frown, shocked that he would suggest such a thing.

He popped a Unicap into his mouth this time. "I get it," he said. "You never dip your pen in the company inkwell."

He *did* leave the country, sending me postcards from Biarritz and Cannes on his way to Greece. I've been fighting to keep him above-water, but these $1,000-a-month cables to American Express in Athens are taking their toll. His wife, abandoned in the States, has been calling me for money, saying that she cannot put off the grocer and her children's school bills any longer. I can't help her any more than I could help Randolph, and I believe he is not going to come back. His last postcard said: "You can really live big on $1,000 a month here. They are thinking of making me King. The fish is so good I don't need any pills. Where has this been all my life?"

The resident partner saw me reading the card and he saw me smile. "I'm glad you've got something to smile about," he said.

I punched out the symbol of one of Randolph's stocks, which was down about 70 per cent from the highs of 1968.

"That's not a smile," I said to him. "It's gas pains."

8.

Over-the-Counter: Leapfrog in the Asparagus Patch

Tuesday, September 8:

Ginny came click-clicking in today on her spike heels at ten minutes past ten. She carried two large paper containers, milkshake size. One was full of black coffee, the other full of Ted's root beer. Ginny was hung over and late again; but she is the best assistant order clerk in the city. And where can you get a combination of Arthur Treacher and the Playmate of the Month for $125 a week? There is no question in my mind that Ginny is being exploited, but the resident partner still believes in the $50-a-week secretary. (This has nothing to do with the fact that *he* made $211,000 in 1968.)

But people enjoy working for the partner. He is fair and bends over backwards to help his people out of difficulty. We had a registered rep named Billy Bottsford working for us a few years back who had no visible means of support; he barely made his weekly draw against commissions of $100. Yet he lived in a triplex in the most desirable section of town and always spoke of the good things in life: painting, music, fine foods and wine. One day the owner of a restaurant walked into the office and presented me with a bounced check written by our registered rep Billy Bottsford. Another restaurant owner came in the following week with a similar check. (As you can tell, we live in a city where people still believe in the head-to-head approach to good credit.)

I spoke to Billy, and he naturally claimed the claim of all people who bounce checks. "That damned bank," he said, "they've screwed it up again, never credited me for a deposit. This is terribly embarrassing." He told me that I would not be bothered again.

The next week I got a call from the local YMCA, looking for payment for rooms that had been used and never paid for. When I investigated, I discovered that Billy Bottsford had been keeping a room at the Y on a fairly regular basis. I brought my discovery to the resident partner, who pushed back his chair, stared at his wall plaque, which declared our firm to be a Member of the Chicago Board of Trade, and said, "Well," just the way Jack Benny does. I'm sure the resident partner to his knowledge had never known a homosexual in his life, much less employed one. Homosexuals do not gravitate toward finance, at least not to the brokerage industry. Customer's men tend to be hypermale, equating money with power, and with the penis, if you must carry things to their logical conclusion. Even the female brokers are hypermasculine, but that's another story.

The resident partner called Billy into his office and closed the door. The registered rep emerged a half hour later and got onto the phone immediately. I overheard him trying to sell someone shares of Mattel. "If you've ever watched cartoons on Saturday morning," he was saying, "you'd know how these people have cornered a tremendous market. They have assets over $120 million, for God's sake."

I went to see the partner. "What did you say?" I asked him. "I've never heard him try to sell anything so enthusiastically."

"I told him that persecution was a terrible thing, and that I believed that everyone's personal life was his own business as long as it didn't hurt others. Or interfere with their job here. Bill is probably very disturbed, and I told him that we would not tolerate this fiscal irresponsibility. But I told him if he goes to work and uses some of his contacts to stimulate business, he could have a home with us as long as he wishes."

"That was very sympathetic."

"Poor bastard," the partner said. "Probably no one has ever been his friend. God knows how he ever got into *this* business."

Billy did not remain with us much longer. He was incorrigibly irresponsible, and he stayed in trouble with his finances. Nothing large, but enough to leave us with no doubt of his direction. After leaving us, he opened up a restaurant, a fondue house, with a friend in Vermont, where he keeps an excellent cellar and never fails to send the partner a Christmas card. Every December the partner shows me the card and mutters, "Whatever do you think made him go into *this* business?" But Billy is a good example of how the resident partner carries stiffs far beyond where less humane people would have dumped them. I believe the fallen alumni of the brokerage industry could provide enough bodies to staff the State Department for ten years.

Ginny, the assistant order clerk, set her two liquid containers down side by side on her counter, and went to work, dark circles under her eyes. The customer's men would come up to her, hand over orders of slips of paper with over-the-counter quote requests. She would take a sip of Ted's root beer, take a sip of black coffee and phone the various over-the-counter houses in the city to fill the orders and get the quotations.

"How's Viatron?" she would whisper into the mouthpiece, sounding like Judy Garland after an all-nighter. "Come on, come on." she'd say. "I don't have all morning." Then she'd get the quote and yell out. "Five to a half."

Roz the Ruthless called a client back, gave the quote and came back to Ginny with an order to buy 1,000 Viatron at 5⅜.

"What are you going to do," said Ginny, "chisel for an eighth?"

"I put my orders in where my customers say," said Roz.

Ginny swizzled some root beer around in her mouth and called the over-the-counter dealer back. "Freshen up the

Viatron for me, will ya," she said. "Still five to a half? I've got stock to buy at ⅜, anything doing?" The answer came back no.

Ginny called five other dealers, all of whom had an inventory of Viatron stock against which they would buy and sell. This constitutes "making a market" in an over-the-counter stock. The dealers who make such markets list their names, telephone numbers and approximate prices they have traded in the "pink sheets," the list provided daily by the National Quotation Bureau showing almost every traded over-the-counter stock and the people who do business in each stock. Ginny shopped around and managed to buy 500 of the 1,000 shares wanted at 5⅜. Roz persuaded her client to raise the bid on the remainder, and Ginny polished it off at 5½, calling the dealer to whom she had originally gone. "Okay you bastard," she said. "I'll take 500 at a half. See where patience can get you?" He must have said something about where he would like patience to get him, because Ginny crackled a dirty laugh. "Not on your best day," she said and dropped the phone onto its cradle. She finished off the root beer and coffee simultaneously and flipped them into the big metal container next to the Teletype machine.

"All right, gentlemen," she called out to the registered reps at their desks, "you're slowing down. How about some action and some orders?" The production in our office tended to increase in proportion to the size of Ginny's hangovers. Think about that one, Professor Galbraith!

Trading over-the-counter can be dynamite for several reasons. The first reason is the lack of available information on thousands of low-priced issues someone may want to buy or sell. In many cases a company cannot *afford* to publish financial or corporate information, and if you write the company directly, the majority of these firms never respond.

The second problem for an over-the-counter investor is the pricing system of the dealers. Of course, the basic idea in understanding stock trading of any sort is the auction system, the bid on the part of the potential buyer, the offer on the part of the potential seller. When Ginny got a quotation on Viatron that came out "5 to 5½," it simply meant that the dealer would bid $5 a share for Viatron stock. And *pay that price* to a seller. Conversely, the dealer would sell stock (offer stock) to *you* at $5.50 a share. This is how he buys and sells against his inventory. The Viatron pricing was typical of the quotation in an active stock. But for a security that either is traded rarely or is in short supply, a quotation might be 5 to 6 or even 5 to 7. Meaning that if you bought stock at 7 you would *immediately* have a 2-point loss if you turned around and wanted to sell. In good times, with booming markets, one capable over-the-counter dealer can steal more in any one day than all of Sherman's soldiers in Atlanta stole in a week.

With all of the disadvantages of trading in unlisted stocks, the vast majority of small stockholders *only* get tips off the boards. This is because there are almost fifty thousand over-the-counter companies, many of them tiny and local and — most attractive of all — cheap. When you call your broker and say to him, "See what you can find out about Superior Syringe selling around 2½," and he says he'll call you back, this is what happens: he checks the pink sheets for approximate prices *and* to find out how many dealers have an inventory in the stock. The more dealers, the more active a market, and the better job the broker can do for his customer in buying or selling. Then he checks the big Moody's *Industrial Manual* for a corporate history and a current picture of sales, earnings and business. Usually, for forty thousand of the fifty thousand over-the-counter stocks, there is no listing at all. Too small. Then your broker will check the Black Book — the *National Stock Summary* — for a brief listing of the company, telling the address, transfer agent, original come-out price and underwriter. All of this takes three minutes. As a last resort, he'll wire his New York research department and ask: WHAT HAVE YOU GOT RE SUPERIOR SYRINGE OVER-THE-COUNTER? NATURE OF BUSINESS, EARNINGS, ETC. PLEASE ADVISE. The request will be forwarded not to an analyst but to one of the few junior flunkies who look up prices for estate valuations, check on obsolete securities and file annual reports. *He'll* look in the same books, throw out the request and pretend he never got it. That's the great excuse in a mechanized civilization, "I never got your letter" or "I never got the bill" or "No one ever gave me the message."

On the off chance the flunky answers your request at all, he'll say: RE SUPERIOR SYRINGE: NOTHING HERE. SIGNED STAX. ("Stax" is the telegrapher's code for statistical or the research department.)

Then the broker will call the customer and wing it, saying, "Interesting little company. Evidently in syringes for medical and hospital use. If they can make any progress, you might be looking at a $5 or $6 stock. Beyond that they'll have to show some *real* earnings."

"So what do you think?" says the customer.

"You buy a $2 stock, you're shooting crap. You want to give it a whirl, go ahead. But I wouldn't buy 10,000 shares."

"Ho, ho," says the customer, who was going to buy 500. But now, not wanting to appear a piker, he says, "What do you think you can buy 1,000 for?"

The broker has checked the pink sheets and sees that most dealers are offering stock at 2½. He says, "Most dealers are offering stock at *two and three-quarters*. Let me try to squeeze it for you."

This is a classic stockbroker ploy, at least with smart stockbrokers dealing in over-the-counter stocks. They will quote the stock to the customer ¼ or ⅜ or even ½ point over the *actual, real* market at the time. There are two reasons for this. First, it is a safety valve for customers who *always* put orders in for stocks below the market, even if they absolutely want to buy. If a customer believes he is being a cute trader, the broker is being one step cuter, assuring himself of the order, and assuring that the customer will buy the stock.

The second reason for jacking up the price is to make the broker look good. You tell a client, "The stock is offered at 2¾. I'll try to squeeze it for you," then you call the first dealer, buy it at 2½, stall for a while and ring the customer. "I shopped around," you say, "and managed to buy it all at 2½." The customer is thrilled with the execution, you are thrilled with the commission, and there is no way for anyone to be the wiser, because there are no time checks for the over-the-counter dealers. And, since every dealer is his own private mini-exchange, no one quite knows where he stands at any given instant. The same situation in reverse can be used with people trying to *sell* stock.

Now why all the verbiage concerning Superior Syringe? Because customers expect their brokers to be bottomless wells of information on *every* company traded, both here and abroad. The truth is that almost every broker knows a handful of stocks *really* well, the ones he is recommending currently. Dozens of others he remembers fairly well from having traded them in the past, and possibly two hundred or three hundred more he knows by name and product. More than these four hundred or five hundred companies — forget it. But a customer — everyone for that matter — likes to feel he is doing business with a winner, a hero. And winners know all fifty-three thousand publicly traded stocks, right down to the last quarterly earnings and the names of a few directors. You can't say, "I never heard of Superior Syringe." Customers want to believe in you. When I was training in New York one of the partners told me, "Always have an answer, son. You can change the answer later. But always have one. It's like looking busy in the army or always acting as if you *belong* everywhere you go. Your clients are paying for information and answers. We are the closest thing to show business in the business world, and we've got to give the audience what they want. Be vague if you want, but give them answers. No one remembers the guy who said 'I don't know.' He's out in Teaneck pushing doorbells."

Another pitfall in trading over-the-counter that I must point out is the *principal* trade. It is legitimate, under

NASD (National Association of Securities Dealers) regulations, to *mark up* the price a customer pays for a stock by 5 per cent. What does this mean? It means that a broker can call an over-the-counter dealer, buy a stock for you at 20 and send you an invoice at 21 *net*, no commission showing on the confirmation. If you bought 100 shares of a stock on the Big Board at 20, the commission added would be $27.00, of which your customer's man would get approximately one-third, the remainder going to his firm. If your customer's man bought you 100 shares of an over-the-counter stock at 20, marked it up to 21 (the full 5 per cent) and sent you a bill, the commission you would pay would be $100. He would get 50 per cent of this, or $50 — again the rest going to the brokerage firm.

Take this a step further. Assume you buy 100 shares of a stock on the New York Stock Exchange selling for $100 a share. The regular commission would be $49. The same stock over-the-counter, and marked up 5 per cent to $105, yields a commission of $500. If you call your broker and question the fact that no commission shows on your confirmation, he might say, "Right. It's all included in the price. I bought it for you at $105 *net*, commission added." Most customers don't question it beyond this explanation, and if they check the newspapers for prices, chances are the over-the-counter stock they bought is not even *in* the newspapers. There is room in the papers for only the best-known, most actively traded unlisted stocks. Another reason to tread lightly when you cannot even get a daily check on your merchandise.

If you ever get a confirmation from a broker showing no commission and he tells you it is included in the price, question him on it. Almost all of the larger member firms of the New York Stock Exchange do business in over-the-counter stocks *only* on an *agency* basis: that is, charging the regular New York Stock Exchange commission. This avoids temptation and gives the customer, if not a fair shake, at least the knowledge that he is not paying an inflated price with an unreasonable charge for services rendered.

Another safeguard instituted by most major firms is the policing of orders in cheap stocks, stocks selling under $5 a share. Many firms make their customer's men mark their order tickets in such stocks UNSOLICITED, taking the firm off the hook in case the unlisted stock goes down the drain. It also supposedly eliminates "bucket shop" techniques of peddling cheap stocks to the unsuspecting but greedy public. If you mark your orders UNSOLICITED, it means the idea originated with the *client*. It means that the broker did not promise pots of gold from the gold-mining stock in Utah that you got the word on and which sells for 1¼. Because *everyone* will buy 1,000 shares of a stock at 1¼, and if some salesmen I've known are turned loose with a tip like that, they could wind up controlling 50,000 to 100,000 shares like breaking sticks. Then it's a case of the old Georgie Jessel story of the broker who sold him thousands of shares of a penny mining stock. Each hour the broker would call Jessel to buy more, and each hour the stock would be higher. Finally, after starting in the morning to buy at fifteen cents, the afternoon comes and Jessel owns 20,000 shares. The broker calls at two-thirty, "The stock you bought and kept buying is up to $1.50," he says. "Great," says Jessel, "sell."

The broker pauses. "To who?" he says. End of joke. But not the end if you're loaded with a dog.

Marking orders UNSOLICITED *is* a joke if you know your client. They'll all flip for a cheapie, and they all will sign the letter your firm sends them that attests to the fact that the order was indeed unsolicited. Jay Gould would turn over in his grave if he ever saw such a letter.

Another safeguard for the public is the restriction by large major brokerage firms against accepting *any* order for a stock selling under $1. The usual reason put forward is that the public should not be speculating. The *actual* reason is that we lose money on most of these trades. It costs us practically $35 for *every one* of these confirmations, buy *or* sell, that you receive when you trade with brokers. We lose money on every trade where the commission is less than $35. This is why there was a big move on Wall Street to eliminate, or restrict, the activity in small accounts. But the public will find a way. When the markets heat up again, they'll be back with both feet. People resent things done for their own good, and it holds true for history as well as for the New York Stock Exchange.

I must point out that cases of marking up stocks and giving inflated quotations are isolated symptoms of the industry, and not general practices. My purpose in acquainting you with them is to make you more professional in your dealings with *any* stockbroker.

If you ever had doubts, there are *clients* who are sharpshooters also. "Chiseling bastards," brokers call them. Brokers who get caught in these situations. But let me illustrate: I was playing squash a few weeks ago, and after I finished, I walked into the club steam room. Lying face down on one of the benches was a stockbroker I know from another house. He had a towel over his head but I recognized him from his rear end, purported to be one of the largest in the industry.

"What's the matter, Dan?" I asked him. "You looked tired."

He sat up. "I've been reamed by a chiseling bastard," he said. "Bought him 300 shares of a New Issue he asked for seven months ago at 12. It's now 3, and he calls me up, says he wants his money back because it's not blue skied in the state, and he doesn't have to pay for it. It's going to cost me $2,700, which I don't have, that chiseling son of a bitch."

"Blue sky" laws exist separately in each state and cover the registration and sale of a particular stock offering in that specific state. Technically, if you buy a security not registered, or blue skied, in that state, you can renege on the purchase. Sneaky but legal. In the steam room case, a customer requested a broker to get him a stock, which the broker, acting in good faith, did. No one bothers to check blue sky lists, not for 300 shares, anyway. When the stock went down, the customer racked his brain for an out, most likely supplied by one of the countless sleazy attorneys who make their living by suing brokers, doctors, and husbands. If the stock had gone up, you can bet your pre-Castro Upmanns that there would have been no retreat to the state house to check blue sky registrations. Fat Daniel, you may be sure, will be damn careful of the over-the-counter stocks he buys for customers in the future.

What can you do to become more adroit when trading or buying over-the-counter securities? First of all, be sure you trade with a member of the New York Stock Exchange. In this way you will be charged regular stock exchange commissions and not be handled the way you are handled by decorators, furniture dealers, car salesmen and other types who pin your tongue to the roof of your mouth with their markups over cost. Smaller, localized brokerage firms are on the way out, so be careful of them. They are in a capital squeeze because of the large costs of doing business in the industry today, and you don't want to get caught with your stocks and money being held in their hands. Class-action suits have a way of being terribly unsatisfactory and lengthy. If you do business with a customer's man whom you like at one of these local houses, tell him to move to a national firm. It's one thing to shoot crap with the stocks you buy; why let it ride with the boys who are not going to be around tomorrow?

One way to test your broker is to ask for his firm's latest financial statement. All of the major investment houses publish these for their customers to peruse. If your house does not have this readily available, you'd better look elsewhere for a broker.

In trading these stocks, caution your broker to shop around. Make sure he tries more than one over-the-counter dealer to obtain the best price for you. And please avoid those stocks which have only one or two dealers making a market in them. If you have only one or two people with an inventory in a stock you want to buy, they'll hammer you over the head. And it's worse if you want to sell. If you have 1,000 shares to unload, one of these dealers may take 100 shares, another 200, and they'll drop their bids on you so fast that you'll realize the education has not been worth it.

One of our direct lines to an over-the-counter dealer rang around lunchtime today. Ginny picked it up. "They've got some Viatron at 5⅜ now," she yelled to the office. "Any interest?"

"Forget it," came the response, practically en masse.

Everybody knows that when an over-the-counter dealer calls *you* with stock at a certain price that they are offering for sale, the stock is about to go lower. They are one class of people who *never* do anybody any favors.

Sure enough, at two-thirty I had Ginny check Viatron with the same dealer.

"It's 4½ to 5," she said. "The bastards saw it coming."

I think someone took Ginny to lunch and bought her a drink. I smelled Scotch in back of the order desk, and it wasn't coming from Benjy's brown paper bag with his ham sandwich and banana.

"Have a good lunch, Ginny?" I asked her.

"Finnan haddie and two double Dewar's," she said in her clipped accent. It was nice to have a queen working on your order desk. Mother Courage who'll fight on your side for quarters and eighths.

You know that old routine that goes, "There are one hundred bars in this town." And the chorus answers: "*Yayyy*." "But they're all closed." Chorus: "*Booo*." Well, that's exactly the way we get reactions in the stock market.

The *Wall Street Journal* claims that "It's the most optimistic mood in many months."

"*Yayyy.*"

And Wright Patman has been urging the Chase Manhattan to cut the prime lending rate from its current 8 per cent.

"*Yayyy.*"

But hijackings by Arab guerrillas are getting serious in the Middle East.

"*Boooo.*"

And by Monday, September 14, it looks like a strike for General Motors at midnight.

"*Boooo.*"

We are constantly whipped into a frenzy by the news media. Because of communications systems far more sophisticated than any known in history, we get instant replay on every disaster that occurs from Bel Air to Beirut. Perhaps we are becoming immune or semidetached in our emotional reactions. I know dozens of people who refuse to listen to news broadcasts on television. "Everything is too depressing," they tell me. Well, personal reactions may vary, and perhaps we are becoming hardened to instant-replay tragedy. But this kind of news still plays havoc with the financial markets, and you can never be too sure anymore where you stand for the long term.

A few principles to bear in mind when trading stocks in relation to the news: *When the market is good, bad news tends to be discounted or ignored totally. When the market is bad, adverse news accentuates the dips, and no one pays any attention to items of a positive nature.*

You can be sure also that the market always goes to extremes in both directions. Prices on companies you may follow will always go beyond, sometimes far beyond, any reasonable level you can predict for them. When they are going down, stocks can always be counted on to go much lower than you believed possible. And they always go down faster than they go up, but I'm sure I don't have to tell you about that.

Week beginning Monday, September 21:

Morgan Guaranty reduced the prime rate from 8 per cent to 7½ per cent, and all the other banks begin to fall into line. Bob the Bear called right after the news to reiterate his posture on the market and to short 3,000 Deltona (a Florida land developer) around $27. "Everything is dropping 10 points in three months," he said. "The government is grabbing at straws, and all debt-structured companies are going to Q. Read Weiss's *The Money Squeeze* so you know what is going on now. It's going to be worse than 1929."

"What do I do, Bob?" I asked him. "I've got to do business every day. I'm on the firing line."

"Save yourself, man," he said, always frantic to make the next call to his next broker. "Save yourself. The first rule of investment survival."

I have a fastidious client who is a pleasure to deal with. He always pays on time and always saves his confirmations and monthly statements. Many customers make brokers' lives hell around tax time in February and March making us dig through records to find duplicates of everything that anyone has misplaced or thrown away during the year. I had bought him 200 Dennison at 14 in June. It was 20¾ today, and he called to say he wanted to enter a "stop loss order" at 20 to sell.

Let's clear up some misconceptions about "stop orders" that supposedly protect the investor in the event he is not calling his broker every five minutes for prices. I have *never* yet seen an investor *or* a speculator who used stop orders effectively. I do not think they work for the average person. Stop loss orders to sell, entered on the specialists' books, protect the stockholder from falling markets. They are devised to limit losses and to protect profits. If you own a stock selling at 22 and you place a stop loss order to sell at 20, you are protected in this way: should the stock drop to 20 or below, touching 20 or any point under triggers your order, making it immediately "at the market." This theoretically limits your loss (if you *bought* this stock at 22) or protects your profits in a falling market (if you own the stock at 15).

If the market slips and the stock trades at 20½, 20¼, 20⅛, 19¾, and never actually touches 20, you are still protected. Once the stock goes *below* your limit (it does not have to actually touch the exact figure), it touches off an execution. In this case *your* price would be the *next* sale after 19¾ (the first figure *under* the triggering figure). Stop losses can be used for all Big Board stocks.

On the American Stock Exchange there are *no* stop losses. Only the "stop limit," of which you must be careful. With a stop limit, the falling stock must hit your price *exactly* in order for there to be an execution. Take the same prices as the stop loss illustration: 20½, 20¼, 20⅛,

19¾. There would be *no* sale of your stock in this sequence, and no protection, because the stock did not trade at $20 even.

In the over-the-counter market, there is no mechanism to protect yourself one way or another — only the *mental* stop loss, which is when your customer says, "Watch it. When it drops two points, *if* it does, sell it."

And you say to your customer, "Okay. I'll watch it. And you watch it, too, in the papers, in case I get busy and don't notice it." In this case the stock usually drops 5 points without your remembering. Then you find out, you don't call the customer and you sweat, hoping the stock will bounce back 3 points where you can sell it. Usually, it falls another 5 points and you lose the customer. But mental stop losses are as fallible as the mind itself.

My advice concerning stop orders for all you people with 100 shares or even 500 shares of an issue is this: if you're concerned enough to be thinking about stop orders on a specific stock, don't be a misguided sophisticated investor — sell on the way up; *sell* at 22. Why give away at least 2 points on the way down? If you've got only 100 shares, if you've got 500 shares, it doesn't make sense to give away 10 per cent. As a matter of fact, it's stupid. Because the pattern repeats itself endlessly. The market drops; the stock falls to 20, and you get stopped out. At which point the stock immediately recovers to 22½ and the specialist has grabbed your stock and you're not sure whether you've done something smart or unbelievably dumb.

"The average investor is a shmuck," the senior partner of one of Wall Street's largest investment banking firms once said in the bar at Oscar's when I was milling in the lunch crowd trying to catch a pearl or two as it fell from his lips. "The average investor is a shmuck," he said, "but the average investor who uses stop losses is a shmuck with earlaps!"

Wednesday, September 23:

I'm beginning to receive tips on the stock market for the first time in nine months. The phones are beginning to ring. At noon the market is up 7.32 to 754 and Dow-Jones announces a cease-fire in Jordan with the guerrillas. A general cheer goes up in the office, and I defy you to name a business, except possibly the Manned Space Center in Houston, where spontaneous cheers go up from the workers.

A lawyer called me who has lost a lot of money in the last year. "I'm glad of a cease-fire," he says. "I don't want *anybody* killed, even Arabs. Except stockbrokers."

It is the first day of autumn.

9.

The Stockbroker as Shrink

Monday, October 5:

The firm managed to break even in September and the resident partner's morning handshake was dry for the first time in months. "We need $90,000 a day in commissions to break even on operations," he told me. "Maybe at last we can get some leverage on the upside. If I can only get rid of this damn cold."

"There is no perfect human condition," I told him.

And Benjy the order clerk piped over his Teletype one of his helpful hints.

"I have the cure for any cold," Benjy said. "The perfect gargle. One-half tablespoon salt; one-half tablespoon Arm & Hammer baking soda; one-half tablespoon Borax."

"Borax is poison, isn't it?" asked the partner.

"I know," said Benjy. "I use Karo syrup instead of Borax."

"He's a classic," said the partner, going into his office to write orders. He's beginning to buy the airlines heavily: TWA at 15, Pan American at 12⅞. Even though he hasn't been in an aircraft since he took a girl on a seaplane ride in 1949. Ten minutes for $8 around Sebago Lake, Maine.

Unemployment this month was the highest in seven years, and Wild Bob the Bear is jubilant. "This rally (the market now stands at 776) is a duplicate of 1930," he says. "It's all over until 1972. No one is paying attention to the General Motors strike, and it's put one hundred thousand people out of work. That's one hundred thousand consumers, and it's going to knock hell out of the economy. Take AT&T. Why for Christ's sake, there is $540 worth of debt behind every telephone in the country; it's the worst company on the board. The government has been lying in the newspapers. They're printing money and they're broke."

Donald Counts was gleeful today, and for a change it had nothing to do with either his father-in-law or Asamera Oil. He has a customer, an osteopath, written up this morning in the newspaper, charged with lewd and lascivious behavior. He had traded heavily in commodities, finally being shot down by a wrong move into copper to the tune of $3,700 in three weeks. Shortly after that he began sunning himself with a girlfriend (a clinical psychologist) on a roof porch outside his apartment. They were both nude and would occasionally get carried away by the benefits of the ultraviolet rays. Many of the neighbors watched and many more called the police.

"You drive your clients to strange ends," I told Donald, who had clipped the item from the paper.

"Commodities can drive *anyone* to strange ends," he said. "Besides, everybody knows that all psychologists are crazy."

The most important rule of all in the brokerage business is New York Stock Exchange Rule 405 — Know Your Customer. But, as I have had occasion to note before, you never *really* know *anyone* until you have dealt with his money. This brings complications. People become terribly involved with their money, and because we brokers are in the middle, they become terribly involved with us. I want to tell you about some of the people and situations I have dealt with over the years which have almost driven me into analysis. Almost but not quite.

I handle the portfolios of at least a dozen psychiatrists. My experience as their shrink had led me to believe that when the time comes that I begin to feel that I'm losing my grip, I will take one or two alternate escape routes: either to feudal Portugal, where a man can be free in the feudal sense of the word (freedom to me is being the lord), or the ultimate freedom, the little yellow pill for which there is no antidote. America's answer to all problems, the analyst's couch, is not for me. Handle their money for a while, go into their homes for social events, and you will have to agree. But have a sandwich before you do.

The first step with a customer is to establish the *need*

factor. He may not want you, but he *needs* you. And if you fool him into believing you represent either a superior intelligence that can give him profits *or* a superior sensitivity that can give him solace, he's hooked. Or she's hooked, and off you go toward that big capital gain, the green light opposite Jay Gatsby's dock

I met a man at a club of mine a few years ago who told me, over the time it took to finish two drinks, that he had devised a computer terminal for small businesses and for educational use that would revolutionize the teaching of math at secondary schools. I was impressed with his intelligence even though he was a name dropper of the first water. According to Mr. Willis (his name), he was being considered as next ambassador to West Germany, was the youngest colonel in the U.S. Army Reserve, had been decorated in Korea, and was an expert in, and consultant to the White House on, China policy. This in addition to being intimate with senators, congressmen, industrialists and the Aga Khan. He was a member of the club, not a guest, was divorced but had three children, and made me feel that I was privileged to buy him drinks. Which I did.

"Do you ever buy securities?" I asked him.

"Knowing technical fields as I do," he answered, "and being privy naturally to many high-level decisions, I must admit I have had my share of opportunities. And winners."

"Let me give you my card," said I.

"Let me give you *my* card," Mr. Willis said. "It's buff and blue, as is my company stationery. Buff and blue, the easiest colors on the eyes, as proven by a test I conducted at MIT."

Every time I saw Mr. Willis in the club after that, he'd grab me for a drink and a conversation. But his conversation was always interrupted by the loudspeaker paging system calling him to the telephone. He was a very busy man.

Willis called me one day at the office to give me names of high officials in our state, especially the state auditor, who he claimed had been primed to receive a call from me and was eager to send me business. *No one* is this good a friend, and I was naturally suspicious. But one of the great customers to have in this industry is someone who will bird-dog for you; someone who gets you clients by mentioning your name, long and loud.

I called the state auditor a couple of times, but he was always out. So this proved nothing. What concerned me was that with all of Willis's conversation, with all his contacts, he had yet to give me an order of any kind.

"Open up accounts for me," he finally said one day, "and one for my corporation. It's time we made a few moves. I want to begin with around $15,000 in each account for a starter. In the meanwhile, how about coming up to the shore for dinner?" He was a great one for sudden invitations to dinner. I'd get a call from his secretary five minutes before I was to leave the office. "Mr. Willis," she'd say, "has laid on a leg of lamb and wants you for the evening. Six-thirty for cocktails."

I refused four invitations a week, and they came at times that seemed calculated to insure a refusal.

Finally Willis gave me some orders, or rather he said, "Buy me $15,000 worth of stock and ship it to *this* bank." (He gave me instructions). "I want you to use your discretion. But I want growth situations."

If you ever want to defraud a brokerage firm *or* a young unsuspecting stockbroker, this is the classic situation. Look affluent and act knowledgeable. Walk into a strange brokerage office and spend a few days there watching the tape and nodding a lot. Perhaps take a few notes on a small note pad or diary, preferably of English manufacture, because brokers are impressed with the English and with real leather accessories. Finally, request a few quotations or some earnings-report information on very volatile stocks: IBM, Digital Equipment, Disney, Corning Glass. Then pick out a broker, either the biggest producer in the office, who will be too busy to pay much attention to regulations, or the newest, youngest broker, who is hungry and will bend the farthest in ignoring the rules just to get an order and a commission. Then play the broker like a marlin. Give him an order for 100 American Research and Development and pay on the third day (you are allowed five days). Sell it the following week and buy 200 Leasco Data. Again pay for it before the due date (the value date). Sell it the next week and insist on your payment on time. By this point you have established that you are authentic, sophisticated, an excellent credit risk and — above all else — potentially an active trading account.

Next time in the office you put an order in for 1,000 XYZ (*you* name the stock) at 50. "It's time to make my move," you tell the broker, who falls all over his Dingo boots getting the order to the clerk. Now you tell the broker you will check with him later, and you leave the office with two possible plans of action, because you don't have a sniff at getting $50,000 to pay for the transaction. If the stock goes up in the next five days, you sell it. Then you take the buy and sell confirmations to a bank or a finance office, or a loan shark, show them the orders with the obvious profit having been made, and work a deal. Believe me, there are banks in *every* city who lump more abuses than you can believe under the heading General-Purpose Loan. Different lending agents require different pieces of the action, but they will pay for the stock, or rather give you the funds for the purchase. You then cross checks with the brokerage firm and pocket the difference. You've taken a "free ride," less interest or vigorish or whatever you call it in your neck of the woods.

"All right," you say. "Fine. But what if the stock goes *down* in the five-day period?"

If the stock has not gone up in five days, you sweat a little. Your only satisfaction is knowing that your broker is sweating a lot more. He's also trying to get hold of you, phoning every fifteen minutes, because you always paid *early* in the past, when you bought $2,000 or $3,000 worth of stock. Now you buy $50,000 worth of stock and not only do you not pay, but you are suddenly unavailable. Of course, you know what's going on with the stock because you're sitting in another brokerage house in another part of town watching the tape. On the sixth day, stalling for your luck to change, you call the broker.

"I've been out of town on business," you say. "I'm sorry,

but it was rather urgent. I'm sending you a check today. Please put through an extension, and I'm sorry for any inconvenience this has caused you."

"Quite all right," the broker mumbles and enjoys his first dinner and good night's sleep in three days. His faith is restored in humanity and in his own ability to judge character.

But you don't send the check and you duck the broker's calls for another two days. You paid 50 for the stock and it's now 47. You call the broker. He wants to put you on to the manager of the office and says, "We're going to have to send you a sell-out telegram."

You get irate and threaten to close your account if they invade your privacy with inflammatory Western Union messages.

They back down, apologize, agree to hold off on any telegram, but wonder out loud where the check is.

You say you're going to stop payment on the *first* check and hand-deliver a new one the following morning.

"Are you in at eight-thirty?" you say, giving them a final zinger. They can do nothing but mutter, "We *can* be in at eight-thirty." The young broker who took your order for 1,000 shares would stay there all night with a blanket, saying his prayers.

Why is the young broker so nervous? Because for any loss incurred in a trade that is no good, *he* is responsible.

When you don't show up at eight-thirty in the morning, or even at eleven, the brokerage firm knows the jig is up. They sell out the stock at 47, and the loss is roughly $3,000. The young customer's man, who cannot reach you *any-*

where, is threatening murder when he finds you. He is now left with two alternatives: either he can have the loss taken out of his pay until the $3,000 is made up (because he obviously violated Rule 405 — Know Thy Customer), or he can say good-bye, Charlie to the brokerage firm and make *them* eat it. In either case, *you* have said good-bye, Charlie to them all, days ago. Easy come, easy go, you shrug, and catch a flight to another city to find another innocent broker greedy for commissions.

This is the classic case of how sharpsters defraud brokerage firms. And it's what raced through my mind considering the possibilities of Mr. Willis and his trading account. What if he isn't named ambassador to West Germany? I thought. So I called Willis and told him, "Look, I think the market is a little vulnerable right now." ("Vulnerable" is brokerage jargon for when you don't really have a clue to what is going on). "I'm not going to concentrate the funds in one or even two stocks. I'm going to buy several situations and spread the risk. That sound all right with you?"

It did, and I was greatly relieved. What I was doing was protecting the firm and protecting myself. If I bought several odd lots in various companies, I was not in much danger if Willis was a no-good. I could sell him out and any loss would be minimal. This would obviously *not* be the case with 1,000 shares of one stock, or even 300 shares of this, 400 shares of that. Willis and I were feeling each other out; this happens often with new customers. It's very much like a first date. When no funds were received by the fourth business day (a few years ago four days was the rule) I was sure I was right about Willis. I called him again.

"How soon are you going to want that check?" he said as soon as I said hello.

"It's due today."

"Do me a favor and put through an extension," he said. "I've got a meeting with the heads of the Boards of Education in Connecticut, New York and Pennsylvania. And Bill Scranton, I believe. I can't get over to see you until tomorrow. By the way, we need a financial man on our team. Would you be interested in joining the board of directors? You get on the corporate letterhead. Buff and blue."

While he was talking, I was madly punching symbols on my Telequote machine to see if any of his stocks had gone down. One who knows what an extension is, is no stranger to the stock market.

On the day we were to send a telegram to Mr. Willis if the money was not in by one o'clock, his secretary waddled in with a check. "Mr. Willis wants these stocks shipped to the bank immediately," she said. "He said to tell you that he's using the securities as collateral for a deal. And by the way, he wonders if you could come up to the shore for lobsters tonight? Bill Scranton *may* be there, and certainly the state auditor."

Willis was of course bright, but crazy. It turned out that he had conned the bank out of $15,000 on the *promise* that he was going to deliver $15,000 worth of fully paid securities to them. He led three local banks down the primrose path this way, and they all told me later that Willis seemed the most charming man who had ever defrauded them. I don't think Willis knew what he was doing. Because of his fantasies, he just believed he was owed certain things by society as *his* inalienable right. If he knew what he was doing, he would be in Buenos Aires with a quarter of a million dollars. Subsequently, he virtually kidnapped a girl from her great-aunt's home one night and kept her prisoner at the shore, much as in *The Collector*. I suppose he just wanted to feed her a lobster. But court led to his being committed for shock therapy, to being drummed out of his club, to the final blow: losing his secretary to Mutual of Omaha. And when the bank called me to sell out Willis's holdings, our firm made a net profit of $137.50 after commissions, and we were most grateful.

It pays to observe Rule 405 — Know Your Customer. The amazing thing is that Willis *did* have a computer terminal, as I learned from another club member, who purchased one for his secretarial school. "He was going to get me three hundred programmers per semester to train," the member said wistfully, "but he never delivered the bodies after the computer was shipped and unwrapped. All I can do is plug it in and punch the keyboard. But it's beautiful. Almost like a piece of sculpture. And colorful too . . . all tan and blue."

"Buff and blue?" I asked.

"That's it," he said, "buff and blue. Real easy on the eyes."

Trading accounts are great fun while they last. Most big brokers who got killed this year had concentrated on one or two major trading customers and ignored everyone else. When the big traders burned themselves out, brokers who were doing $125,000 to $150,000 a year previously in commissions found themselves doing nothing. Fortunately for brokers, the big traders will never believe that they cannot beat the system. And they provide our living more than any other source.

In the middle 1960's I had a large trader named Izzy, who was a traveling salesman for an electrical parts company. He was a real drummer in the old-fashioned sense of the word: full of stories and snappy patter, always in new clothes and with a thousand angles for beating the other guy to the sale. He had just moved from a former territory where he had set sales records: Cherokee, Iowa, to Sioux City to Council Bluffs to Omaha, Nebraska, to Grand Island to Topeka, Kansas. "Shit," he'd say to me, "just like Quantrell's Raiders. They'd see me coming up Main Street in my Chevrolet, backseat loaded with samples, and they'd pull down the shades and lock the doors."

Izzy had a few sidelines to pick up pin money. "You try going into Honey Creek, Iowa," he said, "on a Saturday night, when all they've got happening is a spitting contest. Hucking lungers they call it. Well, I've got a little company of mine I incorporated — Vipco. Various Imported Products Company. I've got a big raincoat I had specially made in Maine. More pockets on the inside than Edison has patents. I carry all of my sample products in the pockets. I can go into any bar or cafeteria in Iowa or Nebraska and pull out one of my products and slap it on the bar, and I've got more friends than you got hairs on your body. Like this needle threader (he pulled out a small plastic contraption the size of a mini–stapling machine). Handiest thing for the little woman since she gave up squeezing juice by hand. One night I sold forty needle threaders in two hours at a buck and a half a crack. Vipco brings them in from Formosa for ten cents apiece and it's all gravy for Izzy. I'm thinking of taking Vipco public some day if I can get more damn pockets in this raincoat."

Izzy made me presents of a needle threader and a combination letter opener and magnifying glass and put down $5,000, which he planned to run to $100,000 and quit his job selling electrical parts. Five thousand dollars doesn't sound like much money, but Izzy was determined to beat the market by "day trading." With his $5,000, under the rules at the time, Izzy could trade in stocks with values up to $20,000 on a given day, provided he bought and sold (closed out his position) on the *same* day. It was a sucker's racket, and I told Izzy so.

"But I like to roll them bones," he said, "and I had nothing to do most of the time out West but play the market on paper. I was a winner 80 per cent of the time and figured if I had my money on the line *actually,* I'd be ahead about $17,000." (I should point out that there are now restrictions on day trading. With $5,000 cash you can turn only $5,700 the same day.)

One of our functions is to act merely as an order taker, so I shrugged and let Izzy give it a try. He started by day-trading 500 TWA warrants at 26½ and made $350. Then he day-traded 300 National Video at 54¾ and made $175.

"Hey, hey, take it away," Izzy said on the phone. He

always called me from the road between visits to customers. "I'll need a damn wheelbarrow, baby, to cart the dough to the bank."

But in three months, between July and the beginning of November, Izzy lost a total of $2,300, almost half his original capital. During this time he played only three stocks daily: Control Data in the 30's, SCM in the 40's, and National Video, which had moved in this period from 50 to 78½. Izzy became frantic and tried buying and selling several times daily instead of only once. One day he called me from a Howard Johnson's around two o'clock and wanted to sell everything out and buy 1,000 American Motors at 11⅝. He was giggling. "This is how we'll recoup," he said. "If I don't call you by three twenty-five, sell it out by the close of the market." (The market closed at three-thirty.) I did, and Izzy lost $250 including commissions, which, by the way, had been substantial during this frenzied period. The next day Izzy claimed no knowledge of the American Motors phone call *or* his instructions to me. It seems he had gotten drunk at lunch and did it on a whim. "It cost you $250," I told him. "Are you going to call it quits with this foolishness?"

Izzy was stubborn, but he managed to end the game by falling down the stairs that same night and breaking his leg in two places. I had to send him most of the remainder of his money for expenses, and I visited him in the hospital, where he was in traction.

"Open up that suitcase in the corner," he told me, which I did. "I made some wine at home in the last three weeks. I make fifty bottles of homemade wine in a year," he said.

"Vipco sells what I don't drink. A very profitable division of Vipco. Good stuff." Izzy got stiff very quickly on his own wine, and tried to pull off his johnny in front of his nurse. It was all over for Izzy.

Upon his release he called me. "I'm finished as a stock trader," he said. "My own damn fault. A person has got to do what he's best at, and I'm a drummer. But I've quit my job — sick of travel and I can't save any money. I've signed onto an oil rig off the coast of Louisiana. They'll pay me $17,000 *tax-free* for six months on the rig. Nothing to spend my money on. Nowhere to go, and at the end of six months, I'll have a leg up on that hundred grand."

After four days on the rig, Izzy faked an epileptic fit and was lifted off the man-made island by helicopter. "Are they kidding?" he told me. "Fifteen miles out to sea and the wind blowing so hard you've got to tie yourself into your bed. I lost $300 the first two nights in a poker game, and I could see the $17,000 flying away into the overalls of one of those tough mothers. They are *tough,* let me tell you. So I decided I'd better fall down and kick my legs a little. Going there was the biggest mistake in my life."

Izzy has drifted off the way all traders drift off, but I think of him every time I get an upset stomach from drinking Chianti, and every time I think to myself that I can pick up a fast couple of hundred by timing the market *just* right and catching 100 IBM for the day.

One of my psychiatrist clients called who thinks he's a comedian and occasionally affects a Freudian accent if you can believe it. "But never to my patients," he says. I reminded him of the list of cheapies I sent him in June that he wouldn't touch, which are now up on an average of 40 per cent.

"As the Jewish lady says," he told me, "vat vas, vas."

"I bet you say that to all the boys," I said to him, and he laughed.

Dr. Rosen got information from only one source, his patients, getting what he believed was a bonus for his services. He always questioned people in analysis on their business dealings. Since patients obviously felt obligated to him for more than his healthy fees, they would tell him when companies *they* knew of or were connected with were going to merge, discover oil or uranium, double their earnings or sell out to Honeywell. Dr. Rosen had some *very* good information and picked some *very* hot stocks. His problem was that he couldn't let go. He could not sell. He could only accumulate shares, watch them go up and down, terminate with the patient so that he no longer had the information, and keep the stock in his portfolio until he invariably had a loss.

"You want to watch them go up and down?" I asked him once, exasperated with yet another faded capital gain. "Why don't you buy Otis Elevator and call it a day."

"You really think I have a problem?" he said. "What if it's really *your* problem?"

"*Come on,*" I said. "My business is to make you money, not make you well."

"Next time you think I should sell, push me if you believe it. The trouble is they're always *my* stocks, never yours."

It is most difficult dealing with the average retail customer, especially when you are offering him ideas on securities to buy. Because customers *like* you to call them and keep in touch and to offer them suggestions. But it is a lousy, unsuccessful way to run your money because the brokers end up ticking off ideas until one of them rings a bell. The stock you *originally* wanted the customer to buy is the first rejected because it's a company he never heard of. Ditto second and third suggestions. You rack your brain to come up with something that will tickle his fancy and you finally do and you make the sale. But it's a stock that you're not *really* familiar with and one which you are almost sure is not right for the client. But he wanted to buy *something,* and you're in the business to sell him *something,* and it's too bad that this aimless offering of merchandise has to take place. Because everyone involved will be a little unhappy with it. *You* feel that he has settled for a windup Victoria instead of a KLH; but *he* feels that you have sold him something that *you* know all about and fully approve.

Brokers should not have to reel off ideas until one of them clicks. Customers must become more sophisticated today, because most of the big money is made in companies the average person has no feel for, no knowledge of, and for whom receiving a report on the company will probably only produce more confusion. If they're serious, these customers should have decision-making powers taken away from them. Their money should be managed by someone who does not have to become emotionally involved with a customer who is indecisive: "Should I or shouldn't I?" Okay for Hamlet, but not when you care about your own personal bottom line.

Matters get more complicated by the social pressures of being in a business where you deal with people's money. Dr. Rosen had me to dinner in his home last year, I guess to pay me off for the guilt he felt in not selling Slick Corporation (involved in pollution control) in the high 20's. He had owned the stock from 13 up to 29 and had ridden it all the way back to 13.

"What'll you have to drink?" he asked, expansive as hell in his own home, a modern series of white corridors, chock-full of paintings and metal circular stairways and even a brass fireman's pole for his kids to get quickly from the third floor to the family room (a horrible addition to the vocabulary of the suburban dweller).

"A vodka and tonic, please," I said.

He passed me a highball glass three-quarters full of vodka, one-quarter full of flat quinine from a quart bottle that must have been standing open in a refrigerator for months. I choked a little from the first sip. "What is *in* here?"

"Oh Christ," he said, pushing his glasses back onto his nose. He was constantly pushing his glasses back onto the bridge of his nose, and they would constantly slip back to the tip. "I don't believe in jumping up to make people drinks all night. It's foolish when you're entertaining. So I make sure that one is enough to hold them for a while."

All four of his children stayed around through hors d'oeuvres and drink (note the singular here — Rosen was right about asking for another). And the children kibitzed through dinner, as if it was a bridge party and they were dummy. The Rosen children ranged in age from fifteen to seven, with the eleven-year-old boy constantly interrupting any conversation to ask pointed questions of the guests, including the woman on my right (a college librarian), of whom he inquired, "Have you ever had a nose job? Your nostrils are so big." Dr. Rosen laughed and had more fried rice with bean sprouts (we ate Chinese food on their good china, served right out of the restaurant's white cardboard containers). After dinner the conversation turned to pet charities of the doctor and his guests — all ultra liberals of the country club variety who want to free Angela Davis but whose wives patrol bus stops on Thursdays to bird-dog someone else's black cleaning lady with offers of $15 more a week.

Rosen's kids were right in there to the bitter end, bullying us to play Scrabble with them so they could give the poor guests the final humiliation. But the doctor did have beer in the house, and, as I was sure he couldn't ruin that, I had seven, directly from the can, and I tried to share every one of them with the eleven-year-old, hoping I could get him sick.

"I think we got closer," Dr. Rosen said to me as I left around midnight. "We'll be able to communicate much better."

But this year he's back to his old tricks and has ridden everything down from large profits. Litton, Fruehauf, Baxter Labs, and his over-the-counter stocks, which I won't mention because some of them I can't find quoted anymore.

Tuesday, October 6:

The Dow-Jones average has hit a recovery high from the lows to 782.45, on volume of over 20 million shares. Our firm did $120,000 in commissions yesterday, plus $25,000 in surcharge revenues, plus $17,000 in commodity business.

The resident partner is grinning broadly and has a good word of encouragement for everyone. But the customer's men are not very much affected and their business is not keeping pace with what seems almost completely an institutionally oriented rally.

A customer of Donald Counts's who was on the verge of a stroke came into our New York office to obtain the certificates to 300 U.S. Steel he was worried about not receiving. Customers are still concerned about the state of Wall Street and brokerage firms. Counts's customer owed us $125 on a back dividend to which he was not entitled, and we were not going to release the stock to him until we got paid. If we shipped his stock, we could whistle for our $125. Not much money you say? But you know the old story . . . $125 here, $125 there. It adds up.

The customer went to New York, saw our chief officers by pushing his way in, and then began to scream in the corridor of the twenty-third floor outside our main boardroom until he had a crowd of customer's men and Brooklyn secretaries around him three-deep. He got very red in the face grabbed his heart and had to be led to a couch in the Partners' Dining Room. Another partner ran to the cage (where securities are processed) and our box department and pulled out a "street" (in the firm's name) certificate for

300 U.S. Steel. He ran back, handed the certificate to the customer, and they literally pushed him into the elevator and punched LOBBY. A guy who will scream and yell and cheat you out of $125 is the kind of guy who slaps lawsuits on you for $125,000 for his medical side effects. Whiplash on the twenty-third floor is all we need!

Tuesday, October 13:

The market had been sliding for days with high unemployment figures, the General Motors strike and the relentless rise in the cost of goods and services.

Dr. Rosen called me today and capitulated. "You're right, damn it," he said. "When I get even I'm going to get out. And when I go back in *this time,* I'm going to take profits."

Something had gotten into him.

"I'm going to run stocks up and take those profits," he said. *"If* we ever see profits again."

"So, now vee may perhaps to begin. Yes?"

10.

Going Public: Hot and Cold Running New Issues

Monday, October 26:

A leading financial publication made an astoundingly astute comment today. "Once third-quarter earnings reports are in and election returns known," it reported, "we are likely to see a decisive breakout one way or another." And the roof won't leak if it doesn't rain.

We have been in a so-called *consolidation* phase of market trading for a few weeks, with the averages moving in a very narrow range, 756 to 767 on the Dow. Not much action but a lot of talk, like many people we all have known over the years.

Business and social news continues as bad as it was through the spring and summer: General Motors reports a $77 million net loss for the third quarter, the largest in

its history. Corporate profits are lagging in general, and
it looks like a disastrous fourth quarter to come. I hear
that many small businessmen who always paid their bills
thirty to sixty days at the outside are now taking as much
as one hundred twenty days to pay. This situation, the
slow payment of bills, is what kills small enterprises and
forces so many bankruptcies. Big business is also getting
murdered. Honeywell has laid off eleven hundred people
in Massachusetts and offered to relocate them in Okla-
homa.

"Okay, boys," says Jim Curran about this, "onto the
stagecoach. You'll love the reservation near Fort Sill.
One blanket and all the firewater you can drink."

The industry is keeping their fingers crossed on Goodbody and Company, who are in big trouble. Merrill Lynch
is playing U.S. Marine with a planned $30 million guar-
antee from New York Stock Exchange member firms to
swallow Goodbody and save their two hundred twenty-five
thousand customers. Let's hear it for Merrill Lynch.

Our secretaries could care less, while we discuss the
horrors of the situation and the fact that the *Wall Street
Journal* ran a front page story recently headlined WHERE
HAVE ALL THE CUSTOMERS GONE?

"What was the rebellion of 1262?" one of the girls wants
to know, looking up from her crossword puzzle. She has
just finished reading *Love Story* in the office and was crying recently while she was answering the phone.

"I knew things were bad," a customer told me, "but
don't you think you're carrying it a bit too far?"

"I thought you'd sympathize," I said, "and buy a thousand shares of something."

"I just want quotes from the pink sheets on three of my cancers. All my money from now on goes into *land*."

Tuesday, November 3:

Election Day. The consensus from the customers and the brokers is that there will be a swing to the right, away from the radical liberalism that they say has caused so much social unrest and certainly has contributed to the stock market disasters of this year. Whenever there are unrest and uncertainty, financial markets are shaky; investors get nervous and run for shelter. Traditionally, the stock exchanges are closed on Election Day, but with every nickel counting, we're open, like a family grocery store on Sunday. But God has taken a hand, letting us know that Election Day is probably *His* day as well: our telephones are all out with a cable disturbance; our Teletype is down, and we are getting the usual response from Western Union, who services the machine. They blame American Tel for *their* problems locally; American Tel blames Western Union for *their* inefficiency, and between the two they lick the platter clean and are keeping us out of business. The Dow-Jones news machine is out; the desk-top Telequotes are showing four green horizontal lines on their screens and nothing more. On top of all this the bars are closed, so you can't even get a drink. Perhaps today is the day; the Martians are landing and will make Orson Welles emperor. As to the election: Donald Counts is always full of little-known information. "Nixon is a great poker player," he tells us. "During the war he won $1,500 on a pair of deuces from a commander."

"I wonder who handles Nixon's portfolio?" someone asks.

"Are you kidding?" says Jim Curran. "I understand he has all of his money in German marks and Brazilian cruzeiros. And he's been buying stamps like Franklin Roosevelt."

Sonny Huber, the ex-butcher, took the opportunity of our communications blackout to show me a "deal" someone had brought him. Deals in the brokerage business generally consist of three areas, all falling into the category of corporate finance. The areas that all Deal Makers want to exploit are these: companies wishing to sell out to someone else; companies wishing to *buy* out someone else; and companies wishing to *go public* or to offer their stock for general sale for the first time.

Sonny's potential deal involved raising $250,000 for a company manufacturing specialty gift items, especially candles which would be sold in novelty shops all over the country. "Candle sales are on the upswing," Sonny told me. "And they want particularly to make so-called spoof candles at high markups."

He handed me a few sheets of paper showing cost projections and earning pictures on through the next five years. I love earnings projections for companies that have not yet even been started; they all look so beautiful. But I read on until I got to the place where they described some of their potential products: "Our spoof candles will be terribly timely and keep up with current popular tastes. We are planning candles in the shapes of historical figures such as Spiro Agnew, President Nixon, and Teddy Kennedy.

And more candles in the shapes of bombs, Molotov cocktails and dynamite sticks."

"Sonny," I said, "why don't you go out to your health club, get a message and play some gin. Then try to sell your gin buddies some mutual funds. If this is your idea of a deal, then you'd better go back to putting your thumb on the scale with the ground chuck."

"Look," he said, "the customer told me we could have 10 per cent of the $250,000 if we raised it. Twenty-five thousand. I'll bring in a *toilet* company if the fee is twenty-five grand."

"I'm sorry." I shook my head. "We'll have to pass on this one."

He didn't like my attitude and stomped out to get some coffee without asking if he could bring any back for the boys in the boardroom. Sometimes it's difficult to keep from getting irritated when your salesmen are not paying their own way, especially when the market is in a "consolidation phase." Which means there is no business.

The mystery to many investors about going public in the New Issue area should be discussed. Companies generally sell stock to the public for the first time for one reason — to raise money. This is capitalism in a nutshell. And the money is used to expand their operations; to capture a greater share of a particular market; to delve deeper into research and development. There is also the desire on the part of management to reward their employees and, of course, the little matter of hoping to make themselves rich. Making themselves rich is an interesting consideration, and we'll come back to it, because it was a particular phenomenon of the entire 1960's decade — the boom-and-bust cycle of the New Issue market. Raising capital by selling shares on the open market is a process that keeps our free economy really free. It is a legitimate and desirable process, really the only way a young company can pick itself up and expand, and an older company can keep itself growing. Why borrow from a bank and pay back a loan plus interest, when you can possibly raise the money privately from venture-capital sources? Or publicly from a brokerage firm who acts as an underwriter raising the money for you, then reselling to the public at a profit to themselves.

When a company goes public for the first time, the offering is generally known as a "New Issue." Ordinarily, large brokerage firms have standards for underwriting new company offerings. Generally speaking, the company must have a product in national distribution, or a business with a strong history of earnings and internal growth. Many of the major brokerage firms specify that companies they underwrite must have net earnings after taxes of $250,000 or more, eliminating from consideration those issues which exploit the public and fatten the cuffless jeans of the quick-buck boys cashing in on a fad.

When a company is operating in a glamorous or popular area and receives a tremendous amount of publicity *before* a public offering (thus creating a big demand for the shares), this company becomes a "hot issue." A hot issue represents a *gift of money* to the client, the only sure thing I've ever heard of in any money-oriented game. It's a gift of money because hot issues are guaranteed to go up from the minute of issue, some items having been known to double or even triple in the same day. Hysteria is the cause of this, coupled with our old friends supply and demand. How does this work? If a company is in a popular area as, say, nursing homes have been in the past, and there is a frenzy to bid all companies in this field up, up, up, and you have a chain of three homes with fifty beds in each, and you want to get richer than you are already by soaking the elderly, you go to an underwriter and you tell him you own Golden Age Limited, an expanding company with growth opportunities in the health-care-for-the-aged field.

"Nursing homes?" the underwriter says, biting off a piece of his cigar.

"Nursing homes," you say. "Three of them, but we want to expand. We want to care for everyone over seventy-five in the Middle Atlantic states."

"Are you showing a profit?" asked the potential underwriter.

"Well, not yet. But if we can expand as I've outlined, the numbers can be staggering."

"It doesn't matter what you're making," says the underwriter. "Nursing homes are hot. We'll go into registration with the SEC and be out in three months. How much do you want? A million? Two?"

If you can get public while the country still wants nursing homes, you can sell 200,000 shares at $10 to the public and watch the stock go to $15 the first day. Then you can get linen for your one hundred fifty beds, hire a limousine with an unemployed physicist from Avco as a driver, and look to buy out other companies, perhaps in the hospital supply field. Expand horizontally! Become a conglomerate!

Enlarging this illustration, the small underwriter (and dozens of them spring up when the time is right, as in 1961–1962 and again in 1966–1967–1968) builds up a local enthusiasm for the issue. Perhaps a specialized mutual fund agrees to buy 2,000 shares. Then the underwriter's salesmen tell people that X Fund is taking a *big* slice. "If a fund is buying," the salesmen say, "you *know* the deal is hot. They are professionals." And the orders come in fast and furious, even though the prospectus, or offering circular, has stamped warnings all over it: HIGHLY SPECULATIVE, or INVOLVES A HIGH DEGREE OF RISK. Nobody ever reads a prospectus beyond what the company does, and even if anyone *could* read it, accounting procedures have fallen into such disrepute in the last few years that no one knows what the figures really may mean. You pays your money and you takes your chance.

Two weeks before the offering of the proposed issue, Golden Age Limited, more than 200,000 shares at $10 a share had been asked for; the issue has been oversubscribed. Now the underwriter's people call the customers who have requested stock and tell them: "Sorry, madam, your order cannot be filled for 500 shares of Golden Age Limited. We can give you 100 shares for sure, and another 100 at the offering price *only* if you agree to buy 200 more shares on the open market *after* the stock comes out."

"How does it look for the future?" the woman customer asks, and the salesman takes it from there.

"Would X Fund be taking a major position if the deal were not a hot one?" Everyone wants to be a professional and play with the big boys. The mere mention of a mutual fund as a buyer, and the lady agrees. Tactics like this, multiplied many times, insure the triumph of the New Issue's "after-market," the key to any successful offering of stock.

The after-market is the trading of a New Issue subsequent to its offering price — in the case of Golden Age Limited, $10. If enthusiasm for Golden Age gets so aroused prior to release date, then hundreds of people, shut out of the $10 price due to lack of supply, will buy it anyway on the open market, insuring its rise. This is why stocks that are promoted and offered at $10 to original buyers often open on the public market at $15 to $20 and *keep going.* Hysteria knows no limit on the upside. And the underwriter can pull other fancy tricks if the demand is there; he can raise the offering price to the public from $10 to $12 or even higher if he chooses. Minimum and maximum come-out prices are filed with the SEC, and the final decision rests with the degree of enthusiasm built up around a given stock.

Hot issues are wonderful things for good customers because they are like handing such customers a $500 or $1,000 bill, the reward for producing major commissions in the past for the firm *and* the individual broker. Hot issues are a patronage item, a form of paying someone back *or* of attracting some new high roller with what amounts to a bribe. Of course, with a *really* torrid issue — a Howard Johnson's, a Data General, a Research Cottrell, a Transitron (of sainted memory)—it becomes a status thing, an ego trip, just to obtain *any* shares at the issue price. I remember when Howard Johnson's was the hottest item in America, and our office was given a total of *25* shares to split up and pass out to the three-hundred-odd-customers who had called in requesting stock. So many people called because everyone wants something for nothing, right? Well fine! *You* tell your best customers, 1,000-share buyers, that you have some Howard Johnson's stock for them. Then the issue day they call. "Could you get me 1,000?" they say.

"Not quite 1,000."

"Well, I'm sure of 100, yes? All that business I've given you?"

"I got you 5 shares. The biggest allotment in the office," you say and are greeted by dead silence.

Then: "My brother-in-law, for Christ's sake. He doesn't even have a pot to piss in, got 100 shares from his bank. My big broker gets me 5 shares. What am I supposed to do with 5 *shares?*"

You don't tell him, which is one of the hypocritical areas of the brokerage business. Seldom do I see a major client told off, and too often stockbrokers are treated by their clients like the worst form of sycophant and fool. Most brokers wish hot issues had never been invented, because they can only cause ill will on every side, excepting the corporate offices of the company going public. We as customer's men can never get enough of a hot issue to satisfy the status wish of our clients. The clients grumble about us and move on to brokers who can give them *more* hot ones. We grumble about *our* firms and possibly move on to other companies who do more underwriting. I'm told of a partner of a major Wall Street house who committed suicide during an emotional depression brought on by his tiny allotment of Comsat, one of the most discussed issues of the decade.

Hot issues are more pain than pleasure to us. And for you who call your broker because you just heard about Arthur D. Little and you want some at the issue price, forget it. It's not at all a question of first come, first served. And unless you've traded an average of $30,000 in commissions for the last two and a half years, you don't stand a stock certificate's chance in hell of getting even 5 shares. They're reserved for our *big* clients.

But I'll tell you how you can have your day in court. It means waiting for a while until the frenzied days of Bull markets and hot issues are with us, but you can play with the high rollers until the SEC cracks down on this abuse: the *self-underwritten* New Issues.

Major brokerage firms, as I've said, have certain guidelines governing companies they will take public. Certainly the big firms have their reputations at stake, and they will not consciously put the screws on a retail buyer with unseasoned underwritings which promptly go down. But the SEC allows companies to be underwritten by firms that specialize in promotion, almost to the extent of the old bucket shops. And they allow individual entrepreneurs to bring companies public on their own, using local banks as the collection and subscription agents.

Here's how this works. You're a stockbroker who is very successful, and clients keep bringing you inventions they have patents on, ideas they want capital to develop, exciting concepts they want to bring to market. They are all dreamers who need money to make their dreams come true. But your brokerage firm does no financing of dreams; no "start up" underwritings with companies that have yet to even own office space, let alone have sales and earnings records. This is frustrating to you because you can make more money from one finder's fee or one capital-gains situation than you can in a year grubbing commissions from your Scotch Foursome partners and unsuspecting discretionary accounts whom you put only into secondary offerings of blue chips and utilities. The effort expanded on deal making is more concentrated, but many times more rewarding.

One day a customer comes in with a design for an emission-free gasoline engine, applicable for automobiles and supposedly unlike anything being developed by GM, Ford or Chrysler. "But I need $500,000 to get the prototype built and get things rolling," he says.

You get excited about the prospects and make a deal with the inventor. You will help him raise $500,000 for the engine in return for $30,000 in cash and 100,000 shares of stock in the company for a penny a share. Or two cents a share if you feel expansive. Then you quit your brokerage firm, put a capitalization together, plan to sell 100,000 shares to the public for $5 per share, which will give the company its start. Ecology on Wheels you plan to call it, because gimmick names for hot issues always lend them a certain glamour. You file with the SEC and your preliminary prospectus is eventually approved, with much vomiting I'm sure in Washington when they read what you plan to perpetrate on the public. I can hear the civil servants now, discussing your engine.

"Jesus," says one civil servant, "if I knew how easy

it was to make a killing on the outside, I never would have gone to work for the government. We're a rubber stamp for these guys to steal."

"But we've got security!" says the other civil servant.

That's when they both start vomiting.

Soon your prospectus is approved with items like THESE SECURITIES INVOLVE A HIGH DEGREE OF RISK stamped all over the cover, and with warnings inside like THERE IS NO ESTABLISHED MARKET FOR THIS PRODUCT AND THERE MAY NEVER BE ONE, not to mention other dire messages sprinkled all through the pages of the little white document. But it does not deter you, and you advertise in all the local papers — a tombstone announcement for the offering: *500,000 shares at $5. Ecology on Wheels*, with a coupon to be clipped sending for the prospectus.

The back page of your offering circular is an application which can be detached along a dotted line. Prospective subscribers fill in their names, addresses and social security numbers and mention how many shares they want. Then they drop the application in an envelope with a check for the shares, and you sit back and wait for the agency bank to slit the envelopes and stack the money. The bank holds all funds in escrow until the offering is completed. Then they mail out the stock, along with any refunds to subscribers whose orders cannot be completely filled. On a successful offering you can close the books in three weeks, let selected local over-the-counter houses make a market in your stock, do some further grass-roots promotion to assure the after-market, and you're off to the races. The stock is sold to the new buyers at $10, and enthusiasm pushes the price the first day to $13. Your 100,000 shares cost you a penny a share, $1,000. Your stock on *paper* is now worth $1,300,000. What could be easier? Of course you have restricted, or lettered, stock, and you cannot sell without prior SEC approval. This approval never comes immediately. You must prove your intent as a long-term investor in the company. And this usually means a two- or three-year wait. Possibly even longer. During this time the issue most likely will either sink or swim.

But you can't wait to live like a millionaire, so you find a local bank, or banks, who don't care where their business comes from, and you take a loan against your restricted stock. If the market value is $1,300,000, you may get a loan for $600,000, after you deposit the unsalable stock as collateral. Then the usual pattern with Deal Makers emerges. The one offering was so successful you become an expert; every half-baked concept in popular fields arrives loaded in the briefcase of someone who also wants to become a millionaire. You bring out a company in the waste-disposal field, raising $3 million. A mini-theater movie operation brings in half a million. Almost too small for you to bother. You bring in a million for a new snowmobile company that has been operating out of the men's room of a gas station in Londonderry, New Hampshire.

All this time you are taking penny stock in big chunks and the public is eating up your issues. All the penny stock you are taking to the banks and getting 50 per cent, 60 per cent, in some cases 70 per cent of the market value. Your cash flow is the envy of everyone in town, and the stockbrokers you used to work with hate your guts. Of course you shed your wife, one of the first prerequisites for deal making. "She doesn't know how to handle success," you say. And you immediately marry a young one, twenty-three, twenty-four, who looks great in lynx and goes to a yoga class. You get a new house, a Cadillac with a phone, and an off-duty policeman as driver.

It looks as if you can go on forever when the market collapses. The mini-theaters are burned down for the insurance; fraud results and the stock disappears. The waste-disposal company could never get permission to dump anywhere and plummets from 12 to 1½ asked, no bids. The warmest winter in years forces the snowmobile company back to the men's room. And the banks are checking over-the-counter prices for the state of their collateral. Your ex-wife brings you suddenly to court for nonsupport, and you've spent most of the other monies for the pleasures of life due a successful Deal Maker. The banks want you hung, at the very least. And they, with the other hangers-on, force you into chapter eleven, our American substitute for debtor's prison. You are miserable, but everyone who has wished you ill all along the way is ecstatic. "There's no easy way to success," they cluck, feeling very safe. "There's no substitute for hard work. Hard work, a lot of sweat, and it pays to be a little lucky, too."

So the last generation of Deal Makers disappears, to be replaced by new ones sometime in the next few years when we're back in the golden days when anything goes and there is at least $15,000 worth of venture capital in every doctor's hip pocket, for every purpose.

I had a clue to the top of the 1967–68 New Issue market when a friend of mine told me this story. He and his wife had bought their dream house, an immense English Tudor with lots of rooms and land, but so big as to be almost a white elephant. He bought it for $80,000 — a steal — because the former owner did not want to sell it to the Greek Orthodox seminary that had offered $100,000 for it. My friend was in the house, he thought, for life. One day, when decorating was in progress, the doorbell rang and a fresh-faced real estate agent said to my friend, "Are you prepared to sell your house?"

My friend was insulted by the agent's tone of voice. "Of course not. We just moved in," he said.

"How soon can you move out?" the agent persisted.

My friend was beginning to get angry. "I told you we just bought this house. I have no intention of selling it. *Ever.*"

"Not even for $300,000?" the agent said softly.

"We'll be out next week," my friend said.

The deal was signed, and my friend compromised his dream for the ridiculously ostentatious offer. The $300,-000 bid had come from a Deal Maker to whom money had become meaningless. Three hundred thousand was just so many numbers pieced together. The Deal Maker was worth $8 million, on paper, and was hocked up to the ears. Use this for an axiom: when the pigs of this world are burning $20 bills for their cigars and overpaying for homes (my friend would have jumped at $175,000), then the top is near, the slide is overdue.

My friend's house is now owned by the Greek Orthodox seminary, who could afford to be patient.

A broker who used to work for us but who had drifted

to three other firms in the usual gypsy pattern of this business was an expert at handling New Issues. "When your company gives you all you want of a New Issue, you know it's going to be a stiff," he would say. "And you can never get anything meaningful in a hot one. I tell my clients to take 50 to 100 shares of *every* issue that comes along, because you never can tell. There are always sleepers. And the customer never risks more than $100 or $150 against the shot that he'll make $400 or $500 if it's a good one. And the concessions never hurt."

The concession is a commission paid to brokers who handle the New Issue. On underwritings the customer does not pay a commission; rather, the salesman is rewarded by the underwriter, so much per share for every share of the issue he sells. Thus if the concession is $1 and you sell a customer 100 shares, your fee as a broker is $100. And usually you get to keep 50 per cent of this figure, an added incentive to unload as many shares as you can.

Our ex-broker who specialized in New Issues had said the risks were limited. To a certain extent this is true, because the price of a New Issue is often supported by the syndicate of brokerage houses who bring it out. Most firms will *not* allow a customer to sell a New Issue until after the value date (five days after it arrives on the market). If it's at a premium (*up* from the issue price), fine; if it's at a discount (*down* from the issue price), you can usually get away with a point or a point and a half loss, provided you act quickly to sell on the fifth day. This is what the ex-broker meant by $100 or $150 loss at the most. His theory was that if the New Issue market was booming, a customer, by taking *all* of his broker's underwriting offerings, would catch a few doubles or triples or 10-pointers, and on balance, come out nicely ahead for the year. It's not a bad theory if you work for a good underwriting house. But you need a year of the Bull if you want to cut down the odds.

I had a cute customer in 1960 who thought he'd take advantage of his young broker. The customer only had $1,000, but at that time it was substantial for me, who had only been in the business a short time. He'd call me up and read off a list of hot issues, asking me to get him 100 shares of *any* of them. He gave me no business other than New Issues. This is like calling someone and asking them to send you fifty bucks in the mail, or possibly even two or three hundred bucks. I let him take advantage of me because he could never get more than 10 or 15 shares of the issues (I being low man in the office on the New Issues totem pole), and I did not have many of the ordinary kind of customer who would buy 10 Gillette or 15 du Pont.

He also was cute in the selling of the issues. The day they were released, he'd call another broker, not in the syndicate, who was therefore allowed to sell the New Issue immediately, and he would unload. We would deliver the stock to the other broker, and they'd pay him out. It infuriated me to see him cranking away the profits, $30 here, $40 there, taking absolutely no risk, and acting as if he was doing me a favor.

But I fooled him, because one day he got 100 shares of a stock he had asked for and it came out at 20. And I knew that if *I* got 100 shares of anything, it was the kiss of death. Also, I knew he didn't have $2,000. Shocked when told he had 100 shares, he scurried around to borrow the money, finally getting it from his father, who read him the riot act about speculating, up, down and sideways. He sold the issue out with some other broker at 19½ and breathed a sigh of relief because he could pay off his old man. He breathed a double sigh of relief a week later when the issue dropped to 9½; the syndicate had just dropped their bids and let the stock go to hell. Which happens occasionally.

Then the broker who bought his stock reneged on the trade at 19½, telling my client that he still owned it and they were forced to cancel the transaction because he could not deliver the stock to the buyer within five days. New Issues can take weeks for delivery, and are practically impossible to hand over in the prescribed time limit. My cute trader was screwed, and although he retained counsel and screamed bloody murder, he received no satisfaction and ended up selling the New Issue at 7¾, wiping out his father's loan to him.

He tried to make it up on Brunswick in the 50's; borrowed more money from a friend to buy more at 38 and went for the collar. Whenever I see him now, he looks at me bitterly as if somehow there is a conspiracy against him. I passed him on the street last week with a mutual friend. "How are you doing, Orange Crate?" my friend said to him. When he moved on, looking at me again with resentful eyes, I asked my friend, "Why do you call him Orange Crate?"

"Because he's reputed to live in an orange crate under the $2 window at the dog track."

New Issues can drive people buggy.

GOING PUBLIC: NEW ISSUES

Monday, November 16:

The stock market is still in the consolidation phase, but the General Motors strike has been settled and banks have slashed the prime rate from 7½ per cent to 7¼ per cent. I've begun to buy stocks in the auto replacement parts business, especially Maremont around 9½, which should show a recovery.

I got a letter from an engineer client this morning who has been out of work for four months. It was Xeroxed and obviously sent to dozens of his friends and acquaintances. "Do not hesitate to contact me for anything you need done around the house," it said. "Repairing gutters and screens; minor plumbing, including leaky faucets; painting and papering; even building additions. Nothing is too small, if you will call." Business cards were enclosed, and I got the depressed feeling that has affected me repeatedly over the last two years of the great sadness in the land.

I mentioned this to a few of the boys in the office. Jim Curran said, "They're even killing off Dick, Jane and Spot. Scott, Foresman is removing them from their schoolbooks, claiming they were good enough for the thirties, forties, fifties and sixties but no more. Christ, I expect to see Little Orphan Annie marry Punjab."

A salesman is suing the New York Stock Exchange for violating the Thirteenth Amendment to the Constitution, which abolished slavery. Specifically he filed against the Goodbody–Merrill Lynch merger, claiming it would prevent him from transferring himself and his accounts freely to other brokerage houses. I expect to see an underground railroad soon, smuggling ex-Goodbody brokers to Canada.

The dull week ended with not much volume or business, the averages finishing at 761.57. I stopped into my bank to cash a check, and the branch manager came up to me. "Did you hear about the two stockbrokers?" he said.

"Probably not," I answered.

"The two old brokers," he said, "one of whom says to the other, 'Is it possible to get gonorrhea at 72?'

" 'Why not,' answered the other. 'I got King Resources at 34.' "

I gave him the benefit of a smile and went home for the weekend.

11.

Famous Boy Scouts
Who Died in Prison:
Big Producers I Have Known

Tuesday, November 24:

Benjy the order clerk is like a pack rat. He saves everything. Today he dredged up an old recommended list from McDonnell & Company, who closed their doors this year. "You can see some of the reasons they went Rinso," Benjy said, handing me the list of stocks dated January 1969. They were mentioned in a lovely research package, small enough to carry around in your breast pocket. "For the investor seeking above-average profit," it read, mentioning Wyle Labs at 42½, Hat Corp. of America at 20¼, Felsway Shoe at 27⅞. Now Wyle Labs is 3½; Hat Corp. is 4, and Felsway Shoe is 9⅝. "Felsway has held very well, don't you think?" Benjy said. Working so closely with brokers over the years, Benjy has never purchased a share of stock, and likes to paraphrase Will Rogers by saying that he never met a stockbroker he liked. He puts all his extra money into U.S. savings bonds, waiting for the day when it will once again become a patriotic act.

The stock market and our society seem like patients with a high fever. Either the patient will die or he'll pull through.

I do see signs that the patient is recovering. Our innate sense of humor, for one thing. For instance, an advertisement I see for Emba, the American mink, in a magazine, that says, "So go ahead. Be the first on your block to own a mink during a recession. That's status." And a remarkable happening the other night when I attended a performance of the revival of the 1925 musical *No, No, Nanette.* The audience gave a standing ovation to the *overture,* mind you, when they broke into "Tea for Two." And laughed wildly when the heroine asked for "a glass of milk and some ginger snaps." If I had a phone there, I would have called a brokerage office and bought stock all night, because *No, No, Nanette,* with Ruby Keeler tap-tapping back into our hearts, was the most bullish sign I've seen in a year and a half. It meant the public was fed to the ears with bad news, that they were ready for fantasy, and above all — hope. When they're ready for that, we're on the verge of a big turn in the market. I couldn't wait until the morning to begin hunting for bargains.

Only one thing ruined my evening. I ran into Large Philip, one of the legendary Big Producers of the city. A

Big Producer in the brokerage business is one who generates tremendous commissions. They are usually recognized as such, at $100,000 gross commissions a year, with the most famous reputed to do between $300,000 and $700,000 a year.

Customers and other brokers talked about Large Philip's commissions the way gossip columnists used to talk about Sinatra's conquests. "Large Philip did $400,000 gross last year," people would say, or, "Large Philip spends most of his time in Europe; he has half the banks in Switzerland as accounts and a quarter of Getty's brokerage business."

Philip's detractors would say, "You can take everything that Philip says and cut it into thirds. Then divide *that* in two and you may be close to the truth."

Large Philip was a stockbroker who handled only discretionary accounts. The mere suggestion that anyone who was a customer of his could mention a stock *they* liked, and they would be banished by Philip to another brokerage firm.

"*You* cut leather, Al. *You* go to the shoe show," he would say. "Leave the picking of stocks to me." One can go far in the brokerage business by browbeating or bullying customers. All you need to attract a following is *one* big winner. Everyone will remember you for that one stock. It almost doesn't matter how many accounts you leave beaten and bleeding with your subsequent mistakes.

When Philip came into the business, he had, as a base, the account of his father and the friends of his father, wealthy manufacturers who traded heavily. One of the friends was a Canadian who had had advance word on the mineral find in Timmins, Ontario, made by Texas Gulf Sulphur. Philip bought thousands of shares of Texas Gulf Sulphur, starting in the mid-20's, and kept buying thousands more all the way up to $60 a share. The stock went to 106, then split, and Large Philip began feeding out the thousands of shares he had bought. Legends grow quickly on Wall Street, and Large Philip became a god. "The kid has the balls of a brass monkey," I heard one admirer say about him at the time. "He got me to go on margin at $35, and got me to borrow from a bank at $45, and got me to take a second mortgage on my house at $60. Can you believe it? Mr. Joe Conservative. I made $127,000 on the goddamn mineral strike, and the SEC can take it away from the officers of the company, poor bastards, but nobody's gonna take it away from me. I named one of my kids after Philip. Middle name, but it *was* after him. He's beautiful!"

After the Texas Gulf Sulphur deal, money came into Large Philip by the sackful. He began to take limits on the size of his accounts: nothing under $100,000. Accounts placed at trust departments of banks under irrevocable agreements paid legal fees to get the agreements nullified and the money transferred to Large Philip. "That first year after Texas Gulf," he would say, "I sold out more shit: Telephone, International Paper, Southern California, Edison, Alcan, all that crap that everyone has died with." And he put his accounts into thousands of shares at a clip, selling them out if the stocks didn't go up immediately and going into new situations. If a customer offered his own ideas or even suggested a possible move, Philip would interrupt him. "My secretary handles all discussions," he would say. "I'm going to put you on hold; she'll be with you in a minute, as soon as she handles a cross of 10,000 Butler Aviation."

Getting Large Philip as a stockbroker was like getting Christiaan Barnard to transplant your heart. As it turned out, Large Philip did a lot of lower-intestine and bladder transplants, but that took a while for his customers to realize. I've never known a Big Producer or inventor or industrialist who made his reputation on one stock, or one invention, or one product who ever followed that score with anything but disasters. Not counting Ben Franklin, of course.

One advantage of being a Big Producer is that the rumors that a Big Producer is interested in a stock are enough to get the stock moving. "Large Philip is buying Drektation Electronics," the rumor would start, and people would call their own brokers. It was good for business because Large Philip's reputation made it the only reason people needed to buy Drektation Electronics. Finally, one of his actual customers who had been hustled by another broker would call Large Philip. Phil would be eating a roast beef with Russian dressing on a seeded roll, drinking a black coffee and having a small bag of potato chips at his desk, watching the tape.

"Why the hell didn't you tell me about Drektation Electronics?" the customer would say. "Everybody in town knows you're buying, and you didn't put *me* into it."

Large Philip would spit potato-chip crumbs all over his desk. "I never even heard of it," he would say. "What's it selling for?"

This kind of story made Large Philip feel good; it made him feel powerful and ready to turn 15,000 shares after lunch. Stories about him made him crave more food, and he would flip a quarter to his secretary, who sat opposite him. "Go out and get me an Almond Joy, will you?" he'd say. "Get something for yourself, too." Then he'd wad up his sandwich bag, napkin and potato-chip wrapper, stuff them into his paper coffee cup and arch a one-hander into his wastebasket on the other side of his office. "Two points," he'd say, and swing around to his phone to check his sources for a story he could sell.

Being a Big Producer is like being a money machine, and everyone who becomes a money machine believes it can go on forever. Large Philip gave a party for all his customers and friends at the peak of his production, when he was doing close to $450,000 gross a year. Invitations were hand-delivered by a part-timer from Arthur Treacher Calling dressed as a liveried footman. Each invitation was accompanied by a red rose for the lady. "There are some who would call this nouveau riche," Large Philip said, "but I call it class. And if you don't like it, you can transfer your account."

But, like a Shakespearean hero, Large Philip was shot down by the belief in his own destiny. Every time he sold a stock for anyone he would launch full tilt into a new situation, holding no money back, buying thousands of shares. It is dangerous for a stockbroker to concentrate on one or two stocks, loading all of his customers into them. If something goes wrong, it becomes impossible to get everyone out whole, and you wind up buried under heaps of abuse from clients, and heaps of broken dreams from the remains of your business. Large Philip was running a twelve-room house in the suburbs, a condominium in West Palm Beach, an A-frame in Sugarbush, and a wife with a penchant for Bendels. One thing I'll say in his defense, he was too busy writing orders to care about sex and did no chasing. But since his wife constantly suspected him anyway, he got into the conscience-payoff syndrome, and could say no to nothing she requested. This made him all the hungrier for the commissions he so dearly loved. Feeling he was blessed with the magic touch and a hot hand, Large Philip began to buy an aerospace conglomerate in the 60's for all of his accounts. Sometime later, he finally got the last customer out at 18½.

Getting panicky, he went into a story he received on an oil and gas developer that was rapidly getting into real estate and the entertainment business. Philip liked oil and gas, and begged his people to bear with him, double up on this one, and recoup. He started buying it heavily between 19 and 22, and a client called him who was a talent agent on the West Coast. "I forgive you for the aerospace stock," the agent said. "What the hell, you're not infallible, although you might have gotten out sooner. And you know I like entertainment stocks, so thanks for thinking about me. But *this* one you just bought, forget it. They're producing the worst crud ever cranked out here; they've got to go broke."

"Entertainment business?" screamed Philip, not knowing about *that* division. "They're not in the entertainment business. They're in gas and oil. What are you talking about?"

"Look, Phil baby," said the agent (they still speak that way out in Southern California), "I'm telling you they're in movies up the yin-yang, and you'd better sell my stock and send me a check."

Large Philip had gotten *so* large and desperate to make a comeback that he just took stories on faith and cranked the money into stocks without the slightest clue about what the companies really did. The oil, gas, and entertainment stock was suspended from trading by the SEC, and that meant that all Large Philip's clients could start chanting the prayers for the dead.

Philip's problem, and you can take note of this too if you are having your money managed by a Big Producer, was that he allowed a very personal business to become cold and impersonal. In his dreams of glory, he forgot it was always someone else's money for which he was responsible, not his own. Then the pack turned on Large Philip, calling him every name in the book and backing up the names with lawsuits. Luckily for him Large Philip is dumb, and immune to a certain extent, because he is back operating in a different city and feeling no compunction about calling old customers to solicit business.

Forced to say hello in the lobby of *No, No, Nanette*, Large Philip asked me how business was. I gave him the standard stockbroker answer of the year, "It's been an unbe-

lievable last fifteen months, hasn't it?" Which tells him
nothing.

He slapped me on the back. "Well, I don't know about
you," he said, "but I had both sides of a cross of 20,000
Georgia Pacific today. Separates the men from the boys."

I carefully cut what he said into thirds, divided it in half,
and watched him swagger away. People in the lobby parted
to let him pass, and shrunk away as if the Red Death were
walking among them. They had had enough oil and gas.

David Sawyer was a Big Producer who also had a gimmick: "secondary issues" and their manipulation. Secondary distributions are generally handled like the underwriting of New Issues. They represent large blocks of stock for
sale in companies already public and that most often need a
syndicate of member firms using New Issue marketing tech-
niques for distribution to the public. The underwriter will
distribute the secondary offering, buy the stock from the
seller at 20, and presume to resell it to the public at 21 —
the underwriter's profit being the "spread" between the
purchase price and the $21 sale price. Secondaries are
made attractive to the buyer because he purchases *without*
commission to him. Stockbrokers feel encouraged to sell
secondaries to their customers because of the unusually
large "concessions" to them (so much money paid per
share) for every share they sell. The regular New York
Stock Exchange commission on 100 shares at 15 is $22, of
which the salesman gets one-third to two-fifths. I have seen
as much as $1 concession paid to the salesman on a secon-
dary at $15. Which means if he sells 100 shares, he will be

paid a gross commission (by the underwriter) of $100. Generally he keeps 50 per cent of secondary concessions, a real incentive to get on the phone and get busy.

David Sawyer was one of the few brokers I have ever met who saw the stock market as it really is. He believed that all of his customers were idiots, in the stock market only for quick rides up. And that they all deserved exactly what they got. David believed in squeezing as much out of a customer as he legally could. "What the hell," he used to say. "The customer makes sixty bucks on that trade, and I make a hundred. Everybody's happy when everybody's making dough."

It is a common belief in the securities industry, perhaps even a myth, that a secondary offering, when announced, tends to depress the price of the stock in question. Certainly it does seem to stabilize the stock at a certain level until the offering is completed. But I have never seen a survey (although I would like to) of how prices of companies react before and subsequent to a secondary. Generally, if a stock declines before an offering, the argument is given that management is selling stock to get some money out of the company. If the owners think the stock should be sold, why the hell should anyone else buy? Sometimes this reasoning is valid; sometimes not. But David Sawyer found a foolproof method to big commissions. He would sell short stock in any company with a secondary offering in registration with the SEC. (When you *sell short,* hoping for a stock to decline, you must cover your position, or *buy in,* at some later date to complete the transaction —

just as you must *sell* stock you have *purchased* in order to realize a capital gain or loss.)

David would sell short at 25, for example, when an offering was announced, and cover the short sale by buying shares of the secondary, hopefully at 22 or 23. Not much profit for the customer, except very occasionally when something would fall out of bed on the announcement. But most of the time there was not much risk for the customer, either. And there were tremendous commissions for David, because he'd take advantage of the big concessions the underwriter was paying. A pretty cute trick and one of the reasons David was able to keep above-water this year. "As a matter of fact," he told me, "I'm having one of my best years, because I'm trading on a point profit or loss, sometimes a point and a half. The market isn't supporting moves much more than that, and I want to prove that I can squeeze blood out of a stone." Very few registered representatives can take such continual revenge on their fellow-man. "But I'm like P. T. Barnum," he said. "I give 'em what they want. Wasn't that P. T. Barnum?"

When he wasn't shorting stocks into secondary offerings, David was using them as hammers on his clients, as a reward for his giving them hot New Issues. "You take 200 of this utility on a secondary at 30," I've heard him say, "and I'll get you 100 Pop Art, a really tight issue. You'll make 6, 8 points on Pop Art, and I'll get you out of the secondary immediately. You lose commissions, probably, and that's all. I can't justify to the partners giving you all this hot stuff unless you take some of the junk, too." People would always go along with this bribe. They could understand a net profit of $500 to $600 with no risk. David always knew who he was dealing with.

This is a Big Producer who never, or seldom, loses a client to unnatural causes, because he seldom takes a chance. He's really a small-time chiseler who operates on big-ticket items and keeps the ball rolling, being able to turn over a $10,000 account fifteen to twenty-five times a year. His firm knows what he is doing, but they turn their backs on it because of David's production figures and his absolute insistence that his customers know what he is doing all of the time.

"He's a very strange, secretive man," his office manager told me once. "Won't spend any of his money, won't go to lunch with the boys. With all his big production he's probably very nervous and very unhappy. You can't spend twenty-four hours a day figuring angles on cutting corners to skin a dollar and be very happy. Figuring these little angles for commissions all the time will drive him bananas."

In the meantime, David Sawyer is figuring little angles all the way to the bank.

"You gotta spend money to make it," Charlie Freeman used to say. Charlie Freeman was in his middle twenties when I knew him and making $60,000 a year as a registered representative. He was called affectionately See You Socially Charlie Freeman, because every time he finished making a sales call at night, in someone's home, he'd leave and say, "Good-bye, folks, see you socially." Charlie was a bachelor and spent 25 per cent more each year than he made. But he had expensive tastes: his suits were made by Dunhill, his ties by Meledandri, his shoes by Gucci. Charlie's gimmick was romancing the institutions, where the big blocks were. "I'd trade a hundred retail customers, with their bitching and moaning about 'where is my last Woolworth dividend check,' for *one* institution. Why break your back for the nickel-and-dime stuff? More dough falls out of my bathrobe on the way to the john than half the brokers in your office make in a year with all their old ladies and their dumb businessmen who don't know their ass from first base."

Charlie was arrogant and despised the journeyman stock-broker who made his hard living from the general retail customer. He spent $50 a day on long-distance phone calls to institutions in Los Angeles, Detroit and Chicago. And to company presidents in stocks he invested in. He'd think nothing of calling the chairman of the board of a company and telling him, "Look, I'm about to control the proxies on 100,000 shares of your company. What do you say we have a lunch and talk turkey. You want to meet me in New York? *Lutece? Twenty-One?* Or *I'll* come to *your* shop."

"Who is this again?" the chairman would say, not sure he had heard what he had heard.

"Last chance for lunch, or you hear from me in a different way!"

"Why don't you drop out to my office. Say Thursday?"

Then Charlie would see the company, drop names and $200 or $300 on presents for the chairman's secretary, brandy for the chairman, dinner, and his own plane tickets. He'd come back to his office, pick up a phone, and call eight or nine mutual funds. "Just had dinner with Chairman X of XYZ in Houston" (or Miami, or Louisville). "Here's what you can expect in the next year. Buy the story and you owe me $500 net a month for twelve months. More stories will cost you so much a month, and exclusives, with no other fund knowing, will cost more." Two or three institutions were regular buyers of Charlie Freeman's services, one in particular, where someone who passed out business liked Charlie's presents very much, especially when they came in unmarked envelopes and contained cash. Or when they involved women who visited hotel rooms and made no noise.

The few retail accounts Charlie handled were all on a discretionary basis; Big Producers cannot afford the time it takes to call clients on the phone and explain reasons for buying a particular stock. But every one of his retail customers received a gift subscription to *Barron's* for Christmas. Mutual fund people he talked to received poinsettia plants that would make Good King Wenceslas blush with envy. But nothing to Charlie Freeman was measured in beauty, or size, or shape — only in terms of cost. He would go to any lengths to accumulate and spend more money than anyone he knew. And if he couldn't accumulate, it would be enough that everyone he saw *thought* he had accumulated. "You drive for show and you putt for dough," Charlie would say. "I'd rather hit a two-wood up the middle, two hundred eighty, two hundred ninety yards, and have everyone cheering at my clothes, than anything else. Life is too short, man; you got to grab for all the gusto you can."

He would go to extremes to do what he considered the chic thing. Once he chauffeured someone's Mark III back from Chicago and could have bypassed New York City very nicely in order to deliver it to its owner in Providence. But not Charlie. It was a Sunday morning, the backseat loaded with the owner's clothes (Charlie was just out of college and was being paid fifteen cents a mile for the trip) and the roads were clear and dry. But Charlie detoured one hundred seventy-five miles to have Sunday lunch at the Brasserie, eggs Benedict and Bull Shots. Certain that he had turned heads all over the restaurant, he sneered his way onto Park Avenue to find the Mark III and all the owner's clothes gone forever. Not actually forever; the Mark III was found a week later on Riverside Drive, looking more like a soapbox derby entrant. "The most expensive eggs Benedict in history," Charlie laughed when he told me. "What the hell. The guy can buy and sell you ten times over and never blink an eye. But it cost me my fifteen cents a mile, and I lost his American Express card to boot. He was getting bills for months."

Despite the gift subscriptions to *Barron's*, the more business Charlie did with institutions the more he alienated his retail customers. Gradually they all pulled their accounts and moved to other brokerage firms.

"It's enough to *think* someone is an idiot, Charlie," I told him. "But it's something else to let them know what you think. Especially when those people are richer than you, and in a position to do you damage some day."

"Why should I be a hypocrite?" Charlie said. "They're not rich because they're smart; they're rich because they married it, or inherited it." He smoothed his hair down, and flipped a piece of lint from the flared bottom of a pant leg. "Who needs that aggravation? I can get more action in a week with a block from a fund than all the heartache they give you over a lousy thousand-buck loss on a sour trade. Nobody knows how to take losses like a man."

So the Big Producer concentrated on two institutions and was banging away, $3,000 to $5,000 gross a week in 1968 and into the first half of '69. Then portfolio managers switched in one fund with Charlie's old contact going into the brokerage business himself. Charlie still called on the fund, desperately trying to save the account, until one day the new portfolio manager said to him, "Look, all of *our friends* are helping a friend of ours become attorney general in the state."

"What do I care about *your* attorney general?" said Charlie, whose only interest in politics was when he ran for student council, sophomore year in high school.

"All of our friends are donating to his campaign. You've been a *friend* of ours, haven't you? I've seen the commission runs."

Charlie got the picture and he sent $500 to the campaign for attorney general. The candidate lost and Charlie sent the portfolio manager the *Economist Diary for 1970* with the portfolio manager's initials stamped in gold. The fund was one of the bottom ten performers in the industry for 1970; and they cleaned house of all their brokers. Charlie was down to one account.

"You've got to spend money to make money," Charlie stubbornly insisted, and tried to lunch with the chief honchos of his last account twice a week. But the romance had left the restaurants along with the patrons; the gossip of the Street, at bars and over clams casino, was replaced by the horror stories of cutbacks and the brown paper bags. No one wanted to play Charlie's game anymore, and when he'd go to the Regency for a few days to escape, he'd breakfast alone.

His mutual fund account was loaded with New Issues that had gone bad and over-the-counter junk they could not unload. They still liked Charlie and wanted to give him business; but there was no business to give.

"Anything we give out has got to be reciprocity," they told him. "We have to reward people who sell our funds."

"Do you think I'm going to peddle mutual funds? You've got to be out of your mind," Charlie told them. Like the Ant and the Grasshopper, Charlie Freeman had not planned for winter, and he could not knock on the doors of the people he had called fools.

"They're still fools," Charlie told me one day when I saw him recently. He was advertising for a roommate to share the expenses of his apartment, and trading his own account in commodity futures. "They'll always be fools and not my kind of people. When Charlie goes down," he mimicked a French accent, "he goes down in flames."

The only Big Producers still fighting the good fight were the ones whose fathers came to sit in the brokerage board-rooms. Georgie the Pill in our office was still supporting his son Dickie, although in nowhere near the manner to which he had become accustomed in years previous. He'd move some Disney around and some Fanny Mae every week. "But it's like giving the kid work painting murals in the post office. A man can lose his self-respect," said Georgie.

"I could hold my head a little higher, Dad," said Dickie, "if you'd trade 500 instead of 200 at a time."

"You see what a father has to put up with these days?" Georgie said to me. "My son, the Big Producer."

12.

The Ghost of Christmas Past

December 1, 1970:

I'm a real sucker for this time of the year, and especially now that it appears we're getting presents from Washington. Yes, the economic pendulum is swinging back. The money situation, with interest rates coming down, has improved enormously. The General Motors strike is over; the administration seems finally to be aware of the high unemployment; and consumer buying power should be up, at least to judge by the tremendous savings-rate figures we get from the banks. Companies have cut out a lot of fat, which will show up by the middle of 1971 in improved earnings. The director of ITT's pension fund says he "feels great about the market," which makes *me* feel good.

But there are still disruptive influences aplenty. A prospectus was handed to me today concerning a New Issue: 225 million shares of the War in Vietnam, being underwritten jointly by the Administration and the Joint Chiefs of Staff at a price to the public of $120 billion. There are risk factors mentioned to prospective investors, including the fact that no dividends are being paid and "the company has been actively engaged in business for over six years but operations to date have not been profitable." The prospectus is authentic, and it's another reminder of the grim history that has so influenced markets since the beginning of time.

At lunch today while I was searching the stores for Christmas presents and signs of customers, I was almost run over on the street by a motor scooter driven by a chief officer of a public company with assets over $25 million. He had a beard and a moustache and wore striped bell-bottoms, the new corporate image. But the stock had dropped from 20 to 5 in the last year and I wondered what the annual meeting would bring in terms of response to officers in bell-bottoms and face foliage. I have no desire to see Henry Ford with shoulder-length hair or Mr. E. F. Martin of Bethlehem Steel in a dune buggy with a bottle of Ripple in his fist. I want my executives cutting the mustard on the firing lines, not in encounter groups. What would Robert Townsend say if he were almost knocked tail over teakettle by his executive vice-president on a Honda.

"Up the organization," the vice-president would say.

"You're fired," Mr. Townsend would say.

The times are out of joint, and although the market has

just rammed through 800 and is at its highest level since January 1970, I'm still from Missouri.

December 7, 1970:

Pearl Harbor Day. With unemployment up for the fifth straight month, and a taxi strike on in New York, the market rose again, making a total gain over the last eleven sessions of 61.82 points on the Dow-Jones industrial average. Merchandisers are beginning to call on us again: representatives from mutual funds, pushing their product for us to sell, and tax-shelter boys, looking for pickings in what's left of the big brackets.

A "tax shelter" is exactly what the name implies: a place to duck money from Uncle Sam, but legally. Tax shelters crop up in a variety of guises: herds of cattle, citrus groves, dairy and chicken farms, real estate developments, locomotives and jet engines, oil, gas, and mason jars stuffed with twenties and fifties hidden under a tree near your septic tank. Ideally, except for the mason jars, the money you invest in tax shelters never has to be watched. It is managed professionally for you. You invest your money in a herd of cattle, for instance, along with a syndicate of other investors, and because the government pays to subsidize cattle breeding, they offer incentives to individuals to help them out. These incentives are in the form of tax breaks: you are allowed to deduct a healthy portion of your investment from your ordinary income, as well as certain amounts while the cattle age, plus their feed, lodging, and clothing, if any. In addition to these deductions, your hope is that when Monty Clift and John Wayne drive the herd across the Red River you'll be able to sell the cattle at a healthy capital gain (itself taxed at a lower rate). No insurance is given for rustling, but if you are in the 50 per cent brackets and higher, beating Uncle every year is a pretty exciting game. Milk a loophole until it closes; then find another loophole. That's why we pay lawyers and accountants and deduct *their* fees, right?

Oil and gas constitute the most prevalent, the most popular, and the most heavily merchandised tax shelters. Formerly these shelters were only for the very rich. But someone had a bright idea a few years ago of taking advantage of the nation's growing affluence to sell oil and gas programs to the public the way mutual funds are sold — that is, to concentrate on volume. Let *everyone* think he's going to be in an upper bracket and preach snob appeal, so Mr. On-the-move-up who had a hot year and makes forty grand can tell everyone at his backyard steak fry about his tax-sheltered program. People with $2,500, $5,000, $10,000, which used to be peanuts to the drilling industry, were now being courted with promises of 80 per cent of their investment deductible the first year, intangible drilling costs thereafter, not to mention the continuing depletion allowance. "Why the cash flow throwoff is so exciting," they were told, "and we *project* (there's that word again) that $5,000 invested in our program now should be worth around $20,000 in ten years."

"Not counting all the deductions?"

"Not counting any deductions," the representative from the management team says, fingering his attaché case full of explanatory kits, which no one *I* met could ever really explain or decipher.

With the market decline in the last fifteen months, the man who hit one $40,000 hot year now has taken a long look at his oil and gas investment. And he realizes that he needs a lawyer stationed in Denver to explain his rights and a geologist in Colorado to give an opinion on the plot of ground he holds leases to. Then the investor needs a doctor when he realizes the big difficulty in tax-sheltered programs: the deductions are wonderful, but how the hell do you get your capital out? Many people over the last few years who felt they were moving up in the world now find that they'll have an additional write-off on their 1970 returns; their *total* investment in cattle that have frozen and died; drilling money that has disappeared; locomotives that couldn't be leased. Still, they have their mason jars. They can be grateful for that.

At three o'clock today, a man phoned and said his name was Harry Johnson. I'll talk to anyone, so I had my secretary put him on. "Hello, Brutus?" I knew immediately he was either a mutual fund distributor or a tax-shelter man. They're just like car salesmen, inevitably calling you by your first name all through the pitch. "I'm from Texas Tax Timing, Brutus," he said. "I'm in town to see a few of your leading citizens. Know we can do a lot with you people and thought I'd drop into your shop and say hi."

"Hi," I said.

"Figured I'd drop off a few kits and prospectuses. How would that be? Come in and talk to your people — cross all the t's and dot the i's."

"You do that, Harry."

He was in the next day loaded with tax-shelter kits and wearing a skinny tie with a clasp in the shape of an oil derrick.

"First off," he said, "I want to tell you that the stock broker is obsolete; the mutual fund salesman is obsolete. You're going to get all these services in one package in another few years. And *we're* the answer to all those services; the answer for the privileged man with a high ordinary income. Now what is worse than paying taxes in a society?"

"How about communism?" I tried, but it didn't slow down his presentation. Harry's shelter *started* in oil and gas, rolled over into cattle feeding and funneled you into a piece of a $5 million jet engine which the organizers could then lease back to the cattle company.

"You have all the answers," I told Harry. "I'm going to introduce you to our specialist in tax shelters. She does more in this area than anyone else in the office."

I brought in Ruthless Roz, who chews up salesmen like an International Harvester machine.

"What are you, sonny?" she began, "a refugee from the Petroleum Club in Tulsa? Lone Star beer and sixteen-ounce steaks? You trying to sell *me* on tax shelters in oil and gas? Why the North Slope has taken $9 *billion* out of domestic drilling."

Harry had all the figures memorized to debate Roz, but the truth was that she had put fifty clients and friends into drilling syndicates in the past, and all fifty clients had written off their entire investments long ago. Dry hole after dry hole followed assessment after assessment. The clincher came when her richest uncle called. "This kind of tax loss I don't need," he said. "Money in your oil and gas is like pissing off a moving train."

Since then, Roz eats tax-shelter salesmen for breakfast. Harry ended up dropping six of his prospectuses and sales kits and scurrying out the door.

Given the collapse of John King's empire (King Resources), it will be a long time before the representatives of these concepts will get a decent reception in brokerage firms. Many new millionaires, or about-to-be-millionaires, have had to reconsider very carefully their tax positions in the last year. Many of them, with holes dug in their backyards for swimming pools, waiting for the concrete to be poured, are contemplating diving in anyway. I have a client in the construction industry who lost a bundle on a cattle herd. "From now on," he assures me, "I only seek shelter in Scotch whisky."

One of the many booklets praising the glories of investment in oil says, "The thing to remember is that there's a difference between a *loss* and a deduction." It would be difficult to prove this difference to thousands of people who were looking for pie in the sky and found it all over their faces.

Mutual fund assets these days total around $53.5 *billion,* and fund executives are being quoted frequently in financial publications, because of the funds' huge buying power and the fact that on a given day these institutions can account for as much as *half* the trading volume on the Big Board.

"Should I buy mutual funds for my children for Christmas?" a client asked me today, who was terribly concerned about the financial welfare of his offspring. Some parents live only for their children, as if a little piece of *them* dies when their children are born. These parents talk of nothing else; work for nothing else; plan for nothing else. And, as the resident partner is fond of saying, "watch their kids grow up to give their parents a boot in the ass as the kids walk out the door."

The partner is a big believer in self-reliance: his daughter lives in France, totally alienated; his two sons avoided the securities markets, one as an oceanographer with the Smithsonian, the other as a developer of shopping centers with a taste for airline stewardesses. They are all married, but the resident partner never considered buying any of them *or* his grandchildren a mutual fund. "I get pleasure seeing them at Thanksgiving or Christmas," he says. "Then, everyone is festive and forced to love one another. I can be stiff the whole day and have a wonderful time."

The mutual fund industry has grown like Topsy in the last decade and has wrought a revolution in the stock market because of funds' size and influence on prices. When I speak of institutions, I primarily mean these mutual funds, with literally billions of dollars to invest. So far in this book I have concentrated mainly on the fund *people* and this tremendous pressure they generate — directly, through investment, and indirectly, through the rumor mills and the media. But what about the millions of ordinary investors, the people who *buy* the mutual fund shares, who fuel the fund furnaces with those billions of dollars? *I* know very few people who have put a lump sum investment into a mutual fund, *any* mutual fund, over the last ten years, who now have a meaningful profit. I say "meaningful" to give the fund wholesalers time to unravel their charts and comparisons with the Dow-Jones industrial averages, and their statistics proving that $10,000 invested in Hydra or Octopus Growth Fund (...) ll in the fund of your (...)th $111,000.

(...) meet an active businessman who has not eventually become disgusted with (...) most likely he bought (...)t from a struggling (...)ck. Because mutual funds, in the main, are *sold* to the public, the way life (...) (...)ttle pressure, a little (...) (...)r door to buy a fund (...) (...)hattan Fund when it (with the possible exception of Manhattan Fund when it was offered; but I could have an entire book on that sub(...)re book on that sub(...), seldom make calls (...) lazy, seldom make calls (...)ive mutual fund buyers. This despite (...) commissions (the loading, or sales, (...) loading, or sales, (...) purchaser. (...)s charge usually can (...)est of the total amount purchased, (...) 1 to 4 per cent.

(...) of mutual fund salesmen who (...) in a bond from a put-and-call (...)part-timers, who only moonlight in (...) sell their friends and loved ones, then pack in the job, and they are the (...)e insurance salesmen who shove funds down people's throats in a package deal, along with protection for the families of the buyer, when the *buyer* goes to the great beyond. Insurance salesmen I must lump with dentists and funeral directors who join the Masons and the VFW because it generates business. These part-timers give the mutual fund industry a bad name — the only qualification they must meet is to pass an exam given by the NASD (National Association of Securities Dealers), where everyone taking it has access to the questions in advance and which J. Fred Muggs could pass after an hour of tutoring from Joe Garagiola.

Yet despite the many illusions about the fund industry and the many drawbacks to fund ownership (mainly the fallacy of "professional" management and the ignorant tactics of moonlighting salesmen) the mutual fund *can* be useful, in my opinion, in *two* specific ways. First, as a *forced savings* vehicle on a regular basis. By this I mean *specific periodic payments* in specified amounts, monthly, semiannually or annually. Putting fixed dollars into the *same* fund over a period of years, while the fund sells at *different* prices, gives you a chance to dollar-cost average. This method *forces* you to buy when the market is low, when you ordinarily would be terrified to invest. I have a fund plan myself because I spend every dollar I can lay my mitts on. I put away so much every month in a fund, and *double* this amount whenever there is a dip of 40 points or more in the Dow-Jones industrials. Being forced to save money this way, in small amounts and in equities, is the only *successful* way to buy mutual funds I have seen. If you want to put a lump sum into a fund and forget it, *forget it!* You're only going to be fooling yourself and putting a few dollars into the pockets of the guy who hit you for a one-time sale and went back to driving his cab. Investing periodically in any major fund (and many offer these plans with monthly purchase programs as small as $25) you will not be so tempted to liquidate because you're bored with poor performance as the person who put money in *once*. If you're a parent who lives only for your kids, it's a great way to accumulate money for expensive educations, assuming there still will be colleges by the time your children have grown. (If there are *no* colleges, you can buy the kids some bottled air to breathe and some Poland Springs mineral water to drink. Those commodities ought to be quite expensive by then.)

The other reason to buy a mutual fund is for the self-employed person. Under the Keogh Act (HR-10), a federal law, self-employed persons (doctors, lawyers, small businessmen, et cetera) can begin investment retirement programs for themselves *and* their employees, *deducting* each year's contribution to the plan. A wonderful tax arrangement, but the IRS makes it so damned complicated to set up and supervise your own plan you are almost forced to seek refuge in a mutual fund (many of whom have already set up IRS-approved plans). So make it easy on yourself, and let the fund do the work. It is better than paying the tax, and quite simple to initiate. Call your investment adviser, as the radio advertisements urge you. But don't let me catch you thinking that you are going to get rich quick on a mutual fund. Remember, they move by pennies, up *and* down. But if you are willing to be a turtle, with *regular* investments, you're probably going to be a hell of a lot better off than the rabbits who bail out of their mutual funds to buy Hoo-Hah Industries, over-the-counter, and end up shredding the certificates into biodegradable bits. If you're not in mutual funds to put aside slowly, for that rainy day we keep hearing about, then go see your friendly local stockbroker for his firm's current recommended list of stocks. Who knows? You buy enough stocks, you can start your own mutual fund. Free enterprise strikes again!

Monday, December 14:

H. Ross Perot, the billionaire from Electronic Data Systems, is a true humanitarian, airlifting food to Vietnam prisoners of war, and airlifting millions of dollars to bail out duPont Glore Forgan, the troubled brokerage giant with projected 1970 losses of over $16 million. A new game in brokerage boardrooms is figuring out the paper increases or losses every time Electronic Data Systems goes up or down a point. Counting other people's money has always been a traditional American pastime.

Ruthless Roz, our female Bad Man of the Dakotas, has scored again. She and her husband have owned three or four A-frame ski homes, up-country, for investment purposes. "But you wouldn't get me near one of those mountains," she says. "We bought the houses for capital appreciation only. *I* like to be warm; I like Florida. You can *have* frostbite. The only good thing about ski country is mulled wine and the profits you can make from the suckers who takes the properties off your hands. You've got to be crazy to freeze the way the suckers do, just to be seen up there."

But watching her husband go through three winters still learning the snow-plow turn and seeing the big money that people spent on ski equipment made Roz start buying Head Ski recently between 6½ and 7⅜. Sure enough, the Gladstone Gander luck of Ruthless Roz came through today, with AMF Corporation making an offer for all of the outstanding shares of Head Ski at 13½. Head had closed yesterday at 7½. It's now all over the tape at 13, and Roz's triumphant shrieks were magnificent to behold.

"Money breeds money," groused Jim Curran, who had told her just the previous week that Head Ski looked lousy on the charts. Besides, Jim didn't like the looks of Jean Claude Killy.

"How do you like them apples now, Curran?" Roz said, rubbing it in. She sold all of her stock immediately at 13.

What is the story on "tender," or takeover, offers? Why did Roz sell her shares at 13 instead of offering them to AMF and receiving $13.50 per share? Because more often than not, tender offers and merger situations have a way of falling through. When they fall through, the company being bid *for* usually takes a dive back to where it had been. I have always made money taking profits on the runup of a company when a tender or a merger is announced. I've never been sorry that I missed the top, assuming that the proposed deal is finally consummated. Besides, if you *do* tender your stock to a buyer, he may take some, on a pro rata basis, and return the rest. But in any case, if you *do* tender your stock to a company making an offer for your shares, it ties you up for the period of the proposal, giving you no more flexibility or choice. And remember this: if a company makes an offer of $20 a share for *another* company now selling at 10, the stock *bid for* will probably jump immediately to 17 or 18. Why not to 20? Because the stock being bid for will always sell at a discount from the offer price, as a hedge against the deal falling through. And if you get out at 17, and the deal *does* fall through, watch to buy your stock back at 11 or 12.

Why? Compare it to life. Once a girl has been engaged and the engagement gets broken, you can bet your shrinking dowry that she'll be engaged soon enough to someone else. If someone is interested in buying out such a company, it will appeal to a variety of suitors over a period of time; the game will always be on again. As a matter of fact, more money was made on companies in 1967 and 1968 because of merger or takeover *rumors* than was made on any actual consummation. The anticipation is everything; remember that. If *people* have affairs on this basis, why not corporations?

"I think it's time to buy Green Shoe," said Roz. "With my proceeds from Head."

"From one extremity to another," said Curran jealously.

Green Shoe manufactures Stride Rite, one of the better-known brands of children's shoes, and Roz had made money on merger rumors there in the past. "Every time that stock's in the low 30's, I make money on it," she said. "Noise about merger with Kayser Roth, it went up. Noise about merger with Penn Central, it went up. *Somebody* with some bucks will come nosing around again. Once a bridesmaid in this business, always a bridesmaid."

"That has a ring to it," Curran said, watching Roz buy 400 Green Shoe at 30⅞.

Since I check the commission business at the end of each day, I saw that Curran secretly had later bought 100 shares for his *own* account at 31. He grinned sheepishly at me when he left the office and put his finger to his lips. "If Green is good enough for St. Paddy," he said, "it's good enough for me."

I won't dwell on it, but I want to say a few words about so-called "inside information." No matter how closely corporate secrets are guarded, no matter how tight-lipped executives are, you will always see a stock's activity increase before major announcements are made. Stories inevitably leak; some people always know in advance.

A few years ago I got a tip from a neighbor of the mistress of an officer in a Big Board company that resulted in one of the big profit makers of the year, and one of the biggest stories. The merger I was told about never took place, but another one did with the same company, and I was on the horse all the way, like a bear in a honey jar. Or rather a bull in a honey jar. Tips from the bedroom are the only tips I believe.

If you *do* receive an inside story, and it seems to make sense to your intelligence — *not* your emotions — then nibble at the stock. Watch to see if volume picks up in the issue. And after you buy it, be cynical at all costs. You will probably be told something like "Buy XYZ at 10; there's a deal on, a takeover at $20 a share sometime within the next three weeks."

When you're given a tip on *anything,* you are usually told the time element, as all tipsters want to let you know how *soon* you're going to get rich. This time element is almost invariably wrong, even if the tip is correct. And the price is almost invariably wrong also. On a tip like this, where you are told the stock will double, be satisfied with 50 per cent. If the stock goes to 15, run like a thief. Take your profit and send your source a bottle of Chivas. Or a case, if the profit warrants.

There will be a psychological study of stock market

trading someday (I may even write it), and a chapter should be devoted to the *reasons* people give tips to other people. Love, guilt, friendship, insecurity, reciprocity are all good reasons. If only the tips were all as good as the reasons. That's why I tell you to be cynical. You may not always make the Big Score, but you'll usually be around to play mañana. And if you're careful, mañana always comes.

Christmas week:

With the market trading in the 820 area, and our commission business definitely picking up, there is a cheer in the office that is not just artificial because of the tiny trees with tinsel the secretaries have put on their desks. An analyst on the radio this morning said, "Every major Bear market since the 1920's historically has advanced 50 per cent of its losses, then gone on to make new lows. I would be aggressively defensive." But that's what makes horseraces, because a lot of people are looking for business to improve in 1971 and for interest rates to drop even lower. And when the Chase Manhattan cut its prime rate on Tuesday to 6¾ per cent, I even had a customer call and tell me President Nixon was the best thing since the flush toilet.

We've been buying financial companies and insurance stocks and international oils and a new glamour area — textile companies, particularly the double-knit manufacturers, clothes that keep a permanent press: Palm Beach Company, Venice Industries, Devon Apparel, Kay Windsor. It's a new ball game.

I promised to mention before the end of the book specific ways to avoid stock market trading the way everybody trades: a few dollars' profit one year, a few losses the next. Then a *really* good year, followed by a disaster like 1969 or 1970, where you give everything back. Only double!

There are two outstanding ways to make money in the stock market, but they are probably too dull for the average person, who would rather have action than capital gains. The first and dullest way to accumulate a small fortune is to pick two growth stocks, an IBM or a Polaroid, and begin buying them in small amounts, in odd lots, 5 or 10 shares. Every year, and in every *dip* in the market especially, you buy a few more shares. Eventually you add a few more companies, an American Home Products, a Revlon, a Plough, Incorporated, and you begin accumulating *them,* never selling and buying only on dips. This is how you build a portfolio, even with relatively little money to invest. Everyone I have ever seen who accumulated a fortune in stocks operated more or less in this manner. Any stockbroker can help you assemble a representative list to get you started.

The second way to get rich in the stock market is to find a cheapie; something under $5 a share, that you develop a feel for, that you can get close to and believe in. Then, you begin buying: *you take a position in the stock and keep buying it.* This method takes patience, money, and guts. Also you must avoid any outside pressures, emotional and otherwise, in the pursuit of your goal. If your feeling is correct — if the company is in an area that *must* grow, and if the management is solid, capable and *hungry* — you will be proven right. It will take time, and while it takes time, *you* keep buying. The difficult decision is *when* to sell, especially if you build up to 10,000 or 20,000 shares, and the process may take you years. But remember, the IBMs and the Xeroxes are two in a million; you are *not* going to discover another IBM. But if your stock moves, and it goes to 10, then to 20, at every stage you must reevaluate the product. Does it still *have* to move forward? Is the management still hungry? And if it advances further and suddenly becomes the darling of Wall Street, begin feeding it out, *on the way up,* and kiss it good-bye. Just remember that this takes time; the Big Score in the stock market, if you have the intestinal fortitude for it, usually comes along just once in a lifetime.

If it appears that you must trade, and you need to turn your money over, find a stockbroker who has institutional customers, or who places big money with managers who handle only accounts of a half million dollars and up. Because in good markets this is the only information that counts. If your broker is smart, and nimble, he can pick the best brains for you, buying a little cheaper than the funds buy; selling before they unload. Again, on the way up. In the retail end of the investment business, picking a cross section of the best brains is the *most* successful way to run your money. This is true if you *must* trade, week to week, year to year. How do you find a broker like this? This is the problem, said Charlie Chan. But if you shop around, and do your homework, he exists *somewhere* in every city where there is a member of the New York Stock Exchange. But let me know if you find him, will you? I can always use some good information.

THE GHOST OF CHRISTMAS PAST

Week of December 27, 1970:

Christmas came and went, the last weeks of the year usually festive on Wall Street, with nips in the order rooms and long liquid lunches and office parties in varying degrees of debauchery.

THE ONLY BONUSES THIS YEAR, came a sarcastic message up on the Teletype, is, THEY'RE PAINTING THE WALLS HERE FOR THE FIRST TIME IN FIFTEEN YEARS.

The computer used to send up a programmed Santa Claus and trees on the communication system, but even that is cut out this year. Instead, our New Year's messages from the main office consisted of a combination Vince Lombardi pep talk and chaplain's prayer before battle, recounting the incredible year behind us and the future we could hope to expect.

The market has responded to this season of hope with tremendous rallies in the last week; the biggest advances in over a year, and a closing average of 842 on Tuesday, December 29. This is the highest closing level since November 18, 1969.

After trading hours on Thursday, we had our traditional New Year's party: delicatessen sandwiches and the choice of Scotch, bourbon or rye.

"The simpler the choices, the better the party," says the resident partner, laying down the rules.

Wild Bob the Bear called after my second paper cup of Scotch to let me know that he was buying none of it. "Humbug," he said, which was a seasonal thing to say. "We're still short. I can't buy what's going on. The Feds

249

are jerking the economy. It's a mirage and we've got to go back to fundamentals. The truth is going to come out. Talk to you next week."

Every day to Bob is like every other day, and I didn't bore him with greetings of the season.

The New York Stock Exchange volume hit 2,937,359,-448 shares for the year, topping the 1968 record. I believe that we're just scratching the surface, and that by the middle 1970's volume will be regularly over 20 million shares a day. I also believe that the system will make it; that there will always exist the necessity for a marketplace as a release for people's emotional needs. If there *were* no stock market, we would find ways to invent it. In many ways, trading stock is a healthy sickness; and, if it doesn't take itself *too* seriously, an innocent sickness.

Everyone at our party was drinking now, and rehashing the horror stories of the year. It had started to snow outside and the Christmas lights still burned in store windows and around the tops of buildings making us all feel somewhat like children, at least for this once a year. I had another Scotch and watched Benjy the order clerk grinning his rye-and-ginger grin and attempting to kiss Roz the Ruthless on her cheek. A formidable task.

I knocked the big scissors on the side of the Dow-Jones news machine, asking for silence. "A little toast," I said, and everyone quieted down. "All I can think of to say," I said, "looking backward and looking forward, is God bless us, every one."

"Who said that?" said Michael, the ex media rep.

"I think it was William McChesney Martin," said Jim Curran.

"No," I said. "It was me. But I meant it for all the stockholders. And for all their stocks. But above all, for you stockbrokers, for us!"

"I'll drink to that," said Jim Curran.

And we did.

Epilogue:
The Gods' Tennis Balls

Week of April 12, 1971:

There is an old saying that a stiff penis knows no conscience. If this is true, and I have no reason to doubt the wisdom of philosophers, then another statement also is true: stock market investors have no memories. We have been in the valley of the shadow, but the shadow is now behind us, and the days of madness and gladness are with us again.

Albert H. Gordon, chairman of the board of Kidder, Peabody, has this week presented President Nixon with a leather bull "for turning the economy around." The market, in the most amazing reversal ever, stands at 940, up 100 points in the Dow since Christmas, and is poised for assault on the magic figure of 1,000.

Wall Street seems able to absorb the biggest volume days in history so far (on February 8 the market traded 25,590,000 shares); mistakes appear to be held to a minimum; and the rumors now rampant in financial districts deal with suggestions to buy and sell, not with brokerage firms going into receivership. Last July the partners in our firm were poised on the metaphorical window ledges with the daily commissions totaling $27,000 to $33,000. Now the partners are comfortably seated behind their desks and commissions are running upwards of $175,000 *every day*. The surcharge ($15 per trade) figures alone are coming close to the actual *gross daily* figures of seven or eight months ago. We seem definitely to be out of the woods; happy days are here again!

The bars are busy at lunchtime; reservations have to be made for tables a few days in advance. At the offices, personnel changes are frequent; empty desks are filling up; employment agencies are calling; back-office clerks' faces are once again becoming unfamiliar. The beautiful thing about the revolution in the past six months is that not only have prices changed, not only does the economy appear to be picking up, but we seem to be able to *handle* it. The backward brokerage industry appears to be growing up.

Since the prime rate has declined to 5¼ per cent and leading economists (pardon the expression) have generally agreed that business *will* improve as we head into fall, stock market prices have anticipated this, and more.

Just as an example I shall mention a few companies noted earlier in the book, their prices when mentioned, and their approximate prices today. Granted, hindsight is easy. And in hindsight, it really would have been easy to pick stocks, *any* stocks, in June, July and August and make money. The trick was not in the stocks selected (many have more enviable records) but in the fact that they were purchased *at all*. This is the big lesson in this book, and I am thankful that history has provided some proof of the lesson in such a relatively short span of time.

The following table represents most of the actual stocks mentioned or discussed, the dates they were alluded to and

COMPANY	DATE FIRST NOTED (ALL 1970)	PRICE THEN	PRICE AT CLOSE APRIL 16, 1971
Originala	June 4	4½	8⅞
Dennison Mfg.	June 4	12⅞	31
Unitrode	June 4	5	11½
American Bakeries	June 4	10	21¼
Barry Wright	June 4	7½	11
Financial General	June 4	10	15½
Cudahy Packing	June 4	10	21
Polaroid	June 29	low 50's	90
American Sterilizer	June 4	16¼	26
Itek	June 1	36½	51
Cenco	July 1	19½	49½
Allied Stores	Aug. 21	23	36½
May Dept. Stores	Aug. 21	19½	41
Kings Dept. Stores (pre 2-for 1 split)	Aug. 21	15	38
Syntex	June 2	23	53

the prices then, and the approximate current quotations as of the close of business on Friday, April 16, 1971, an arbitrary date, but fortunately for all of us, the point in time when I am ending this manuscript. These companies are used by way of illustration only and not to be construed as any current recommendation to buy. Sorry!

H & R Block is a notable failure, both for my hedge fund clients and myself, who were short the stock around 45 in June. I covered mine in the low 50's, taking a loss when it appeared that Block, during the summer, was the toughest stock to borrow on Wall Street. This meant that the shorts could have been squeezed through the roof. They squeezed me enough up to 51½ and I covered, "nervous in the service" indeed. My hedge fund stuck it out a little while longer, along with some other tragedies they were short which I won't even discuss. The two-edged sword of their hedge concept has turned my clients into neurotic shadows of their former selves. Caught the wrong way for three years, it's now too late to convince their original backers that they have a clue as to what is going on. And, as I said in the first chapter, "20 per cent of nothing is nothing."

The government has taken steps to protect the average investor, creating the Securities Investors Protection Corporation, insuring individual brokerage accounts up to $50,000. And the flow of securities *back* to Wall Street firms for safekeeping has begun. Amazingly enough, through the big advance since fall, the public — the average buyer of stocks — has not really been a factor until very recently. In February, my personal production was well over $15,000 gross, a net to me of $6,500 that month, in total. And at that pace (I can lie with statistics also) I could take home almost $80,000 for the year, less Uncle's share, of course. The other months since December have been comparable. This production has been done practically entirely with institutional customers and managed money, handled on a discretionary or semidiscretionary basis. The customer's men who depend on calling clients and soliciting business are still pooping along, doing better than last year, I suppose, but not burning up any leagues. The odd-lotters are still *selling* daily almost double the amount of stock they are buying. But the institutions are *forced* to spend billions of dollars, forced to follow their "professional-investor" comrades into the breach. Because, once again, their "performance" must be stressed, they can not afford to be left behind.

But recently my retail customers are beginning to call in droves, desperately wanting *something*, because they have missed so much already. Clients and hangers-on now flock to our boardroom seats, passing stories back and forth, buying stocks gratuitously so they can have their chairs back tomorrow. "Buy me 300 Golden Cycle," a customer told me a few weeks ago. Golden Cycle is an over-the-counter stock that was 110 a few years back and got as low as 5¾ in 1970. "Buy me 300 at 15½," he said, which was the asked price at the time. "My buddies are buying it; I've got a good story." He was watching other stocks on the tape go by, the listed companies, and volume was increasing.

"Got it yet?" he said, as five minutes passed. A quote came back . . . "Golden Cycle now 15½–16. Nothing done on the order."

Big Board prices flashed by with the volume figures deleted, a late tape, sign of increased activity and interest. My customer got excited. "Raise it to 16, for Christ's sake, it's getting away," he said, and I did. Another five minutes went by and brokers rushed past his chair to put other orders in. The Teletype clattered and zinged; the phones were ringing. My customer was in a frenzy when the quote came back: "Golden Cycle now 16½–17, market away from us."

My customer jumped up. "I don't care what the hell it's selling for," he yelled at me. "BUY IT!" The tape watchers applauded him and Benjy the order clerk's fingers flew to carry out his instructions. No one remembered the dog days of summer.

We have a few new wrinkles this year, including negotiated commissions on trades of over $500,000. The beginning of negotiated commissions, *if* it spills down to lower levels of trading, will spell the end of the stock market as we know it. Chaos will replace it, and the professionalism the industry has been striving to build up over the last five years will be replaced by price gouging and throat cutting, with investors not seeking the best research or the best service, but rather the last penny squeezed out of an investment house carrying loss leaders. It can only, if it comes, mean disaster for the very people it seeks to protect by negotiated rates — the small investor. I hope the industry spokesmen, in trying to lean over backwards to accommodate the government witch-hunters, do not accommodate themselves into oblivion. No one will do business at a loss for very long, until the writing appears on the wall, or should I say until it crosses the tape.

NASDAQ, a revolutionary system developed by Bunker-Ramo Corporation, now instantly flashes over-the-counter prices, up to the minute, on hundreds of unlisted securities, bringing this vast, unwieldy market under some control, and offering what amounts to a central auction system for these stocks, much like the New York and American exchanges. At the very least, it speeds up the quotation process a thousandfold, and is the most welcome innovation I've seen since the disappearance of the arm garter and the ink rolls for Big Board tickers.

Let me tell you how I know we're in an old-fashioned, pull-all-the-stops-out market. New Issues are heating up. Levi Strauss went public with all their jeans (coming out at 47 and jumping the first day as high as 62) to the most clamored-for offering since Viatron. And the fringe boys are stepping up their activity also. Today I saw a notice that Johnny Weissmuller's American Natural Foods, Incorporated, is going public. I wonder what Jane and Boy have to say about that? "Kreegahh!"

Merger rumors and takeover fever are rising again from their bed of pain. But two of the last few weeks' stories stick in my mind and lead me to believe that I'd better take some profits and salt them away.

A beloved doctor client called anxiously, to buy an over-the-counter stock, 5,000 shares between 1¼ and 1⅜ in a trunk airline company that flew oil people to the North Slope of Alaska. "It's going to 15," he told me with confidence, and an urgency that told me I better buy the stock before it flew away. A week later he called me back. "Dump the goddamn thing," he said.

"But why?" I asked. "You just bought it. You're going to take a loss."

"Sell it," he said. "Their tit is in a wringer. I just got a call from my source. They only have *one* plane. And the creditors have dug a ditch around the plane to stop it from taking off."

I sold his stock at $1, then I fell off my chair in hysterics.

The second tale is also typical of Bull markets. I have a customer who is an employee of a mutual fund. He is a small customer, but he has access to big information; everyone is courting him for business and dropping stories in his lap. He has bought six stocks from me in the last four months and *every* one of them is up *at least* 50 per cent. After the first two, I began riding his coattails, putting my own managed people into the same stocks, after the fund man completed his purchases. If the fund was buying the same securities, I was cutting down the odds; if they weren't, chances are that the stories were being spread around anyway and, if I was nimble, I could take advantage of the runup in price. This week he called me to buy a stock around 11, on the Big Board, that had been depressed for some time.

"What do you think?" he asked me (just for appearances' sake, because he usually had his mind made up when he called.) I thought the stock looked undervalued *if* business in general improves next fall, and I told him so.

"Buy me 200," he said, and I *really* thought he was going to hit it big this time. The stock was depressed; the market was circling around, picking up previously ignored ideas, and, I thought, it had big mutual fund sponsorship. I began to buy the situation heavily for my people, a few of whom know my source.

"Octopus Fund is a big buyer, huh?" they said.

"I don't know if they're buying," I told them, "but all I can tell you is that the guy's track record is great."

I put forty clients into the stock between 11⅛ and 11⅞. Then it started to move up on good volume. When it got to 13¼, I called my original source at this fund. "It's starting to move," I told him, although both of *his* hands were free to punch his own quotation machine. "It's 13⅜ now. Did Octopus take a position? It's kind of thin for you to buy in any large amounts."

"Christ," he said, "I didn't get this from the fund."

"Oh?" I said, not worrying, because my friend had many sources.

"No," he continued. "I got this when I went out to the Coast to see Lockheed, Disney and Pacific Lighting. I was going to Vegas for the weekend, flying from Los Angeles, and I sat next to a guy who gave me the stock. Said it was going to 25. And you'll never guess who he was? Mary Pickford's manager."

"Mary Pickford's *manager?*" I said in disbelief. "You bought a stock recommended by Mary Pickford's manager?"

"He was very certain it would go up."

"See you later. I've got another call," I told him, tripping over myself to bail out all my holders in the stock with a profit — albeit small, but a profit. When strangers on a plane give you a tip that goes up, count your blessings and your beads. None of my customers complained when I told them; they were only amused. Of course, the stock is now 14¼; but people can afford to be amused in Bull markets, especially, I imagine, Mary Pickford's manager.

My office again hums with activity.

Our chartist, Evander Wood, is back on the institutional trail. Institutions once more need the crutch of technical witch doctors and Evander has the fastest sliderule in the business, worn with his fine-point pens in a leather pouch on his hip, low like Billy the Kid.

Sonny Huber is putting money back into his safety-deposit box and giving up his foolish dream of once more becoming a butcher. Michael, my ex media rep, is beating the bushes with some success, hitting doctors, oral surgeons, and law firms with his mutual fund sales kits and his research-department recommended list.

Our husband-and-wife team, Robert and Rebecca, are back in action. They have kept the cleaner and the Lodge brothers alive for the last two years, and they madly flip through their telephone directories, mentioning possible switches out of Jersey into Boise Cascade. Their feet still dangle above the floor, but they jingle merrily now, with new purpose.

Georgie the Pill is trading again, almost weekly, in blocks of 1,000- and 2,000-share lots. His son Dickie has two-hour lunches, with secretaries and female friends of his wife, just as if 1970 had never happened.

Even Asamera Oil has come back, and Donald Counts is allowed to call his father-in-law in New Jersey daily, with quotes and information like, "Well, Dad, the stock is 24⅛, and there's an agreement to explore in southern Sumatra with Mobil and Standard Oil. Dad, how about moving 10,000 shares. Dad! DAD?"

"Did you hear what happened to Helena Rubinstein?" Benjy, the order clerk, asked me.

"No," I said, busily writing orders which were coming in so fast I was now worried about errors, not commissions.

"What happened to Helena Rubinstein?" said Benjy. "Why, Max Factor!"

He broke up, gleeful at his new $10-a-week cost-of-living wage hike to $160.

The American Ping-Pong team has broken through the Bamboo Curtain and the market is strong again, with eight consecutive plus sessions. This thaw in Chinese-American relations is the most bullish news in ten years in its implications for the stock market. Jim Curran says, "I hear they're bringing Bowie Kuhn over to referee the finals."

EPILOGUE: THE GODS' TENNIS BALLS

Just now I got a call from a client who has been gone since March of 1969, buried in one of the longest Bear markets in history. He discusses a certain stock and says he'll call me back, and he calls immediately. "What the hell, I'm loose," he says, "Buy me a thousand."

These are the happiest words of all.

46149